REVIEWS FOR PRACT

MW00445887

**"We become the stories ......
positive or negative tales that shape our reality."**

This book absolutely helped me shift my story. Even with clinical hypnotherapy experience myself, I am still shaken to the core when I really allow myself to accept that my reality isn't really reality - but a million perceptions cause by millions of experiences. I'm still blown away that I went so many years without "God" in my life and now I can see that he's always been there...waiting for me, supporting me and gently guiding me.

If you're the highlighting type, buy extras because there's so much useful content. The exercises they give are quick and so incredibly powerful, I found myself doing them a couple times. I think you'd find a different and powerful outcome every time you read this book. This is a fantastic read for any level of spirituality and experience. It's a true self-help book, no matter your need, goal, or struggle. I highly (very highly) recommend it, and will be strongly advising my own clients to invest their time in it.

\- Cari Moisan, Certified Clinical Hypnotherapist

I had already believed in myself whole heartedly and believed I could manifest all of my dreams but after reading this book I've realized all sorts of thoughts and behaviors that were potentially blocking me. It was easy to read and to follow. I really enjoyed it and the writers did a fantastic job of hammering home the important details.

\- Tyler True

REVIEWS FOR PRACTICAL MANIFESTING

Practical Manifesting is of great value to both the beginner and more advanced student. It lays out the path in a clear and supportive manner, while acknowledging the work involved to become truly awakened. These tools are so difficult to find elsewhere, and yet here they are! It acknowledges the struggle that we all face, and the ability to recognize and overcome it. Following the tools, it is possible to begin, and continue on the path to finding the true joy of our Higher Self. It is a book that I wish I could have found years ago while struggling for this exact information!

Iris has been my teacher for four years now, and I feel truly blessed. Iris has guided me through the past pain that I needed to acknowledge while not knowing it was there, influencing my every thought. With great patience and compassion, she has helped me reach such joy. She continues to help me recognize as my ego self surfaces, and reminds me what I must do to overcome the stumbling blocks that arise. She guides me through meditations that one can only experience while guided by such a teacher/shaman. The awakening of My Higher Self follows a path of commitment and dedication, growing ever stronger and deeper because of the dedication and commitment that Iris has always given freely.
- Marion Thompson

Daniel and Iris offer sound, pragmatic strategies to remove self-imposed barriers to a truly fulfilling existence. Open this book and find your bright future.
- Donna Summers

PRACTICAL MANIFESTING:

Overcome Fear, Realize Truth,
and Create the Life You Were Meant to Live

by

Daniel P. Olexa
Certified Clinical Hypnotherapist,
Life Mastery Coach

And

Iris Terner
Shaman, Behavior Therapist, Spiritual Teacher,
and
Reiki Practitioner/Teacher

MAKE IT REAL.
LIVE YOUR DREAM!

Cover design by Daniel Olexa, Jason Welch @ Earl Design

Cover photo by Abel Escobar via Pixabay

Daniel Olexa's photo by Don Ptashne

Iris Terner's photo by Dale Chan

Practical Manifesting: Overcome Fear, Realize Truth,
and Create the Life You Were Meant to Live

ISBN: 978-0692977965

First Edition: November 2017

Copyright © 2017 by Daniel Olexa and Iris Terner
All rights reserved. No part of this publication may be reproduced,
distributed, or transmitted in any form or by any means, including
photocopying, recording, or other electronic or mechanical methods, without
the prior written permission of the publisher, except in the case of brief
quotations embodied in critical reviews and certain other non-commercial uses
permitted by copyright law. For permission requests, write to the publisher,
addressed "Attention: Permissions Coordinator," at the address below.

Daniel Olexa Hypnotherapy, LLC
PO Box 3161
Redondo Beach, CA, 90277-3161
daniel@danielolexa.com

For Sarah. I am eternally grateful for you. – Dan

For All – I am grateful for the lessons and blessings and to be able to share the same. - Iris

"We all – adults and children, writers and readers – have an obligation to daydream. We have an obligation to imagine. It is easy to pretend that nobody can change anything, that we are in a world in which society is huge and the individual is less than nothing: an atom in a wall, a grain of rice in a rice field. *But the truth is, individuals change their world over and over, individuals make the future, and they do it by imagining that things can be different.*

"Look around you: I mean it. Pause, for a moment and look around the room that you are in. I'm going to point out something so obvious that it tends to be forgotten. It's this: that everything you can see, including the walls, was, at some point, imagined."

– Neil Gaiman
(Italics added for emphasis.)

Table of Contents

Table of Contents

PROLOGUE – Iris Terner

Practical Manifesting is about The Flow, The Way, The Path, but what does this mean?

These sayings are all derived from The Tao, a life philosophy, and for some a religion, which originated thousands of years ago in China. Around 550 BC, a sage named Lao Tzu wrote the first text on Taoism, *The Tao Te Ching ("The Classic of the Virtue of the Tao")*.

Some philosophers and historians believe this ancient structured way of living was already present in Chinese society well before Lao Tzu wrote about it. To this day, Taoism is practiced by over 3 million people.

Taoism promotes a life of complete simplicity, naturalness and living it in such a way that it does not interfere with the course of natural events and what is to be. If we are in rhythm with nature and The Universe, we can attain a happy, pleasant existence. Understanding Taoism is simply accepting your true nature, realizing our True Self, through which you can manifest in a congruent way with the Universe.

Dan and I endeavored to write this book to explain what we have discovered, and continue to discover about The Flow, essential nature of all things, energy, ego and so much more. We discuss the laws of the Universe and how you can find your inner balance so you can *go with The Flow*, realize your True Self, and manifest your ideas in a practical and impartial way.

We offer a range of information regarding healing and releasing negative energy through chakra meditations, changing perspectives, working through ego-conditioned emotional and mental blocks, to help you gain understanding and acceptance of what is The Flow.

Tao Te Ching - Lao Tzu - chapter 37

Tao abides in non-action,
Yet nothing is left undone.
If kings and lords observed this,
The ten thousand things would
develop naturally.
If they still desired to act,
They would return to the simplicity of
formless substance.
Without form there is no desire.
Without desire there is tranquility.
And in this way all things would be at peace.

(translation by Gia-fu Feng and Jane English)

THE PURPOSE OF THIS BOOK

This book is about transformation. It is about rising above your limiting beliefs, finding your True Self and purpose, and manifesting your vision of the possible outcome of the abundant flow of a Universe of Pure Potential. It is about removing the clutter and clatter of that which surrounds and distracts you. It is about energizing you and aligning your inner power so that you may become a co-creator in your life.

In this book, the terms God, The Universe, The Universal Mind, The Divine, The One, The Absolute and The Source will be used frequently and interchangeably. We may also use the gender-neutral term "It" when discussing "God." This is not meant to disrespect anyone's religion or beliefs. Readers will come from a variety of backgrounds with differing perspectives on faith and religion. Our purpose in this book is to focus on what we have in common, underneath the labels. The Infinite has many facets. As human beings living on an Earth full of dualities, we tend to have finite perceptions of our world before we begin to awaken spiritually. As such, we cannot fully comprehend or experience the Vastness from which we all come. We can only sense a small portion of It.

HOW PERCEPTIONS FRAME OUR WORLD

From this perspective, the idea that we can only sense a small portion of the Universe, let us consider how we perceive on this physical plane. The visible spectrum of light exists between approximately 400 and 700 nanometers (nm), within the electromagnetic spectrum. This is the range of visible color that we humans can sense. Ultraviolet light and infrared light exist past their visible counterparts at either end of these ranges.

While we are physically unable to see UV light, we can sense it with our bodies in the form of suntans and sunburns.

More frequencies of radiation exist past these fringes as well. We have created tools to measure these higher and lower frequencies, but we cannot perceive them through our physical senses.

However, within the range of light that we can detect, how well do we sense it? How absolute is the "truth" of what we feel with our physical bodies?

Ask yourself, what color is yellow? It seems like an easy question. Yellow is yellow.

But ask your friends how they perceive color. Choose a series of paint swatches in a range of yellow; see if you and your friends agree on which swatch is truly yellow and which may be some other color.

Scientifically, yellow exists in the spectrum at approximately 570nm. Anything on either side of that is not truly "yellow. Those tones are tainted by green or orange to some degree.

Consider the color orange, yellow's neighbor on one side of the spectrum. It exists at approximately 590nm. Where in those 20nm of variation does yellow become orange or orange become yellow? Every person will perceive these shades of tone a little differently. At either end of the scale, we may have absolute agreement on yellow or orange, but it is in that range that our finite, physical abilities reduce our ability to agree on an exact color.

Are you still not sure that you agree with our illustration above? You "know" what yellow is and all of your friends agree with you? Good. We're glad that you discovered a consensus.

Now ask yourself this question: How does a truly color-blind person perceive yellow? To him/her it is perhaps merely a shade of grey, not the warm, energetic tone that we who are graced with color vision can see. Or, in their eyes, is it an entirely different color? They may see "yellow" as what we would call "green" or "blue."

Is "yellow" still yellow in this case? The light still exists at the corresponding wavelength, but the mechanism by which it is being interpreted is not sensing the light in as the color yellow.

The physical body's senses create limitations which lead to finite experiences of the Absolute. They not only lead to a limited perception of the world, they also lead us to limited perceptions of our True Selves. Much like our experience with the color yellow above, we limit our beliefs about ourselves to that which we experience in the physical world.

We become the stories that we tell about ourselves — positive or negative tales that shape our reality.

PERSONAL PERCEPTIONS

Here is another exercise for you: Write down your perceptions of yourself.

What are you like? Are you a happy person? Are you successful? What do you most appreciate about your life? What words best describe you?

Now write down your perceptions of your closest friends.

What are they like? Are they happy people? Are they successful? What do you most envy about their lives? Ask your friends to perform the exercise for themselves and you.

Now, sit together and discuss your opinions and perceptions of each other. You will probably be surprised to find that you see your friends in a more positive light than they see themselves and they will see you in a more positive light than you see yourself.

Which perception is true? The all are. Your ideas of your friends are no less real than their ideas of you. We are all infinite beings with a multitude of layers, each perceived differently by everyone we encounter based on their experiences and awareness. Each opinion/observation is merely a facet of the overall whole of our being. As we embrace all these aspects of ourselves, we begin to see our true nature behind the outward appearances; we begin to realize that we are the infinite possibilities that are our True Selves.

As you progress through this book, you will realize your connection to the Infinite. Your awareness will grow. You will sense God in new ways and perceive a new relationship with It. You will learn about the principles/laws of the Universe of which your True Self is aware. You will learn how principles/laws function and how to utilize them to realize abundance. This book is about realizing your life of abundance, finding your peace and happiness, and ultimately connecting to who you really are – your True Self which is part of your Higher Self.

Let's begin our journey...

IRIS'S STORY

Everyone has a story... here is mine and how I changed it.

My early years were full of lack: lack of love; lack of food; lack of money; lack of friends; lack of compassion, lack of acceptance, and the list went on and on.

My family immigrated to Canada from Europe right after WWII. I am the second youngest in a family of 6 children along with my parents. I, like most of my siblings, was bullied in school. Children would throw rocks at me, call me horrible names, and would always want to fight to prove that they were better than me. Some would call me at home or stand outside my house to continue their bullying. Throughout most of elementary and junior high school, I felt hated and was an outcast. Thankfully, there were a few children and teenagers who knew better and befriended me.

I understood that these bullies were hurting also because of lack of love in their lives. I would stand strong and face them down or explain to them that they could do no worse to me than what was happening to me at home. Home is where the lack of most good things began for me, because at home, there was no lack of abuse, dishonesty, hatred, and selfishness.

I never actually struggled with the issue of lack of money or material possessions. I had accepted this state of being when I was very young. At the age of four I learned gratitude for what I did have. I knew there were many in Third World countries who had less than my family.

This realization helped me to develop compassion.

My mother stated a few times as I grew up that I had "money luck" because when I needed or wanted something, money would come from somewhere to allow me to buy it. At a young age I shared the little I had with an open heart, giving to others and I would always be "rewarded". It was karma, the cause and effect of the Universal Flow of "what you do, think and say is returned to you".

Through it all in my first 30 years of life, I became angry and struggled with understanding existence in general and people and situations in the world. I found that I had compassion for others and a degree of acceptance and understanding, but I lacked that for myself.

I hated myself!

At an early age I was fortunate to have a strong connection with Christ Consciousness which protected and guided me often, but I did not realize the perpetual flow of higher consciousness until much later in life. This connection was not due to religion, this was due to self-realization.

Yes, so I am a natural born shaman. (If you are not familiar with the term, a shaman is a person who acts as intermediary between the natural and supernatural worlds to cure illness, to act as a seer and spiritual teacher. One who utilizes higher spiritual abilities to do the Great Works of Spirit.)

We all have the capability to realize our true nature and the power of that who we are. I had to go through trials and tribulations to heal and release that which was in the way of my knowing the flow of Spirit/God Consciousness/Christ Consciousness.

The Flow is synchronicity, miracles made known, the creating force and pure consciousness where all possibilities exist. All that I was lacking was fulfilled by The Flow. During the process of my self-realization, I found abundance of all good things and what was meant to be. I also had found the truth of cause and effect of The Flow. This reaches back to many lifetimes, bringing the karma of that which we do not remember that we have done. Karma can be adjusted though.

We are all meant to realize this Truth and connect with the abundance, but only through gratitude, acceptance and self-realization can we know It and be It.

DANIEL'S STORY

Until a few short years ago, I lived my life based on a mindset of lack and limitation. My internal dialogue was mostly about what I told myself I could not do, what I would never achieve and what I did not deserve.

I accepted what was presented to me, occasionally asking for more, sometimes getting it, but mostly not.

I had been programmed to believe that the world was against me, there would never be enough money for what I wanted to do and that happiness was reserved for the successful; my life was meant to be a struggle to merely get by.

Strangely, I had big dreams. I imagined much larger things for my life. There seemed to be no basis in reality for these thoughts. I had no template from which to draw them. I could envision myself as a wildly successful entrepreneur, but I just could not seem to get the right break to earn enough money to leave my day job. For the most part, I was under-appreciated at my work and my ideas for moving my employers' companies forward were met with resistance.

It was a hard thing to accept. I knew I could do better; I knew there was more in the world for me. I was not meant to push paper all day in order to earn a paycheck and just to make it through to the next week. I knew I was meant to have an impact on people's lives.

I felt a connection to something bigger, something that I wanted to share with others.

Until recently, I could not articulate this belief clearly. It was a feeling that I had when I helped friends and even strangers. I could feel it when I linked people together.

You've probably felt the same sensation. Don't ignore it. It is a calling from a higher perspective.

Unfortunately, I was not aware of what this feeling meant. To make things worse, I could not explain it in clear terms.

Language and emotions come from different sides of the brain, so it's difficult to describe a feeling in a manner that does full justice to the experience. There's a lot lost in translation from the left to the right sides of the brain.

The rigidity of words is too limited for the spectrum of emotions.

I struggled to find the reason for my life. What was my passion? What was I meant to accomplish?

I knew it involved helping others to achieve their goals because I enjoy bringing success to others.

But at the time I didn't know how to bring success to myself.

My beliefs in myself held me back.

I could easily see the worth of others but, like most people, my self-worth was hidden beneath my conscious awareness.

Over my lifetime to that point, I had learned lots of negative things about myself and my place in the world. From these experiences, I learned to tell myself that I was not good enough. I listened to friends and acquaintances who said, "Oh, I could never do something like that. It's too scary, too risky." I adopted their fears as my own.

Other times, they projected their limited perceptions and fears back onto me, saying things like, "I can't see you doing that," "You don't know what you're doing," and "There's no money in doing that."

The worst part is that I listened and believed them. I shut down my dreams before I tried to achieve them.

After 25 years in an industry that I loved, I was earning a comfortable income. Not a great one, not a level of income that creates freedom, but a comfortable one; the kind of job that makes you lazy; the kind that makes you think, "I can't leave this job, I'll never get another one that pays like this."

Lesson #1: Comfort kills dreams.

I lived a life best described as quiet desperation. I was married and working at a job I did not enjoy. I was becoming acutely aware of my mortality. At 47 years of age, I began to feel that my options were limited; actually, *I believed* that my options were limited.

As you will learn from reading this book, it is what we believe about ourselves that creates either limitation or opportunity in our lives. What we believe about ourselves is the foundation for the stories that we tell about "who we are".

The story I was living did not match the vision I had of myself. I was confused and frustrated.

My story was not empowering. I lived in a victim mentality that projected the following: I am unable; I am unworthy of being happy; I am unworthy of freedom and security. I am destined for a lifetime of under-appreciated work and never getting ahead.

I was not happy. I was stuck.

Something had to change if I was going to begin realizing the life I saw myself living.

At that time, I had been married for 7 years.

It reminded me of my parents' marriage. When I was in my early teens, I was aware enough to know that my parents should have been divorced. It was not a happy household. I knew then that I did not want to have a marriage like theirs. Thanks to my internal programming, that was exactly the place and relationship in which I found myself.

I think my wife and I were both unhappy, but neither of us had the courage to tell the other how we felt. After months of counseling, I finally had the self-awareness, courage and strength to choose to change my life.

I talked with my wife about a divorce. That was the hardest conversation I had ever had. It was followed by the hardest months of my life as our divorce proceeded. During this time, I told myself horrible things about my judgment and my place in the world: I was being selfish; I should not hurt others feelings just so I could be happier; I was a terrible person.

The voices telling me these things sounded a lot like those of friends and family; like people I had seen who had stalled and given up on their dreams. These individuals were afraid of stepping past the sense of security that kept them trapped in the familiar surroundings of their comfort zone. They chose safety rather than to take a chance on an unknown outcome.

It took me a long time to finally realize that these voices were bullshit.

Lesson #2: Those voices you hear, the ones that hold you back, are liars. They are not helping you by protecting you. They are holding you back by keeping you living in fear.

It was not long before I met a wonderful woman who understood my dreams and helped me become aware that I could actually achieve them! She saw my potential when I was lost. I admired her as well as her achievements. It still means the world to me that this accomplished person saw success in me at a time when I was unable to see it for myself.

It is important to point out that other people are not responsible for our successes or failures. Those outcomes are entirely upon us. However, surrounding ourselves with people who support our efforts and encourage us, rather than those who drain our energy and erode our self-esteem, is a critical step toward success. Making this choice will probably cause you to lose some "friends" or even family members, but you will find yourself in a place where you can achieve your goals at a much faster rate when you release the people who are not helping you to be your very best.

Being with someone who pointed out my strengths and helped me to find my passions was instrumental in the shifting of my internal dialogue from negative to positive. I began to believe in myself and could point to places where I had made a good impact on someone else's life.

I became more aware of my skills as a teacher and problem-solver. I stopped listening to the negative voices in my head that told me I was wasting my time and began to hear a new tone, a new message that said, "What can you do next?"

That support became the foundation for my rebirth - a new me. A more authentic me. I stopped living in fear of an unrealized future and began to take responsibility for manifesting the life that I had been envisioning.

Lesson #3: Helpful, insightful, supportive people will assist you in becoming a better you. They will challenge you to grow. It is not always easy, you may argue, but you will move beyond your limitations if you trust the process.

I took a hard look at myself and the industry in which I worked, commercial printing, which was at that time, and still is, a dying industry. Tangible paper is being replaced by invisible digital pulses.

I had not been happy at my job for years. Yet something beyond just earning a check made me get up and go to the office every morning. I had to find out what that thing was.

I discovered Isaiah Hankel's amazing book, *Black Hole Focus*. It provided the road map for my reinvention. (Go buy it now. You will be glad you did.)

I realized that the reason I went to work every morning was that I enjoyed working with my clients to help them solve their problems. I really enjoyed it when the solution was not readily evident and we had to negotiate the outcome to find the best resolution.

I felt excited by this epiphany! I knew it was true. *Problem solving* was, and is, my passion!

From this kernel of truth, I began to research fields in which I could use my passion; fields where I could have a meaningful impact.

They idea of becoming a hypnotherapist came to me through another epiphany. Seemingly out of the ethers, this idea pulled together so many areas of interest in my life. I had experienced hypnosis and taken part in hypnotherapy as a client, but until that moment, I had not considered it as a choice of career. In fact, at that time, I had just finished a series of sessions with a hypnotherapist in Kansas City. I had gone to her to help me navigate my post-divorce stress and negative beliefs. I saw changes in my attitude immediately after our first session. I was calmer and felt like I had the tools and perspective to live my life differently. I began to re-invent myself.

At first, hypnotherapy seemed like an obscure choice but, the more I considered it as an option, it made perfect sense to me. I had always been interested in alternative healthcare and the role of the mind in both healing the body and creating the environment in which a better life could be created and success could be achieved. I am a firm believer that we will realize that which we focus on in our lives. If you focus on negative things, you will be miserable and pessimistic; focus on the positive and you will be happier and more resilient.

It became my goal to provide guidance to those people like me who felt that they could just not get out of their own way. I wanted to help my clients reframe their beliefs about themselves from limiting ideas to thoughts of unlimited possibilities.

I knew the tagline for my business before I started school: *Whole. New. You!*

In 2015, after completing over 500 hours of training, I opened my office in Naples, Florida.

I was my own boss. I began working with clients around the world to help them achieve their dreams by using hypnosis as a tool to re-frame their negative beliefs into positive, future-paced images of their success. I was using my passion for problem solving to help others achieve their goals.

Lesson #4: You CAN do it. If you can dream it, you can achieve it.

The results have been astounding!

My choices and beliefs in myself were confirmed. I did have the ability to start over, become my own boss and make a difference in people's lives.

I won't say that it's always been an easy path; every choice comes with challenges, but it has been fulfilling on many levels.

My clients have reported major changes in their relationships, health and success. Their stories have validated my belief in myself, as well as anyone's ability to successfully realize their goals.

I made the right choice to break out of my comfort zone and make hard decisions. I am now living the life that I envisioned years ago.

Lesson #5: Just as negative people can drain you, positive people can uplift you. Who you surround yourself with determines your success and happiness. Choose wisely.

As you read this book, please realize that your goals are achievable. Everything happens at its appropriate time. The world is not against you; that is merely your perception due to your experiences up to this point in time. Make the choice, as you read this book, to leave the past behind you. Go forward knowing that as you focus on your goals, you will realize them.

The Universe is on your side! You are still alive and living; your dreams are waiting for you. You will achieve them.

INTRODUCTION

We are, all of us, for better or worse, what we think about ourselves.

Henry Ford once said, "The man who thinks he can and the man who thinks he cannot are both right. Which one are you?"

Thousands of years earlier, Confucius made a similar statement: "The man who says he can and the man who says he cannot... are both correct."

Two men, thousands of years apart, making amazingly similar statements about the nature of belief in one's self and one's abilities. What inspiration can we take from these insights that our thoughts about ourselves create our outcomes?

When you see articles in the media about "How the Stars Are Not Like Us," do you imagine your shortcomings? Do you tell yourself that there is no way you can ever realize such an elaborate lifestyle? I am here to tell you that you can achieve all that and more.

With clear intent, intense focus on the outcome and dogged determination to achieve, you can make anything happen in your life. The only thing holding you back is you and your belief structure.

Let's begin with what we say we cannot do.

OUR NEGATIVE TENDENCIES

For a moment, focus on the things you tell yourself. Do you tell yourself that you are not good enough, too stupid, too fat, too ugly, too poor to make a difference in the world or in your life?

When you try to achieve your goals, what things limit you? What things do you say repeatedly that hold you back, keeping you in a pattern of lack? Common examples include, "Same shit, different day," "It's always the same, nothing changes," "The world is against me," "I just can't get ahead," "Nobody loves me," or, "There is no more opportunity left in the world."

Do you have any others to add to this list? You can write them down in the note pages at the end of this chapter.

Let us take a moment to look at those beliefs. Are they truly logical? If you were to look at all the things that you encounter, both good and bad, during the course of each day, could you really say it is the "same shit?" If you were only focused on the negative things that occurred, and we will talk more about that later, is it all really, "the same?" Probably not.

By focusing on the negative, we tend to over-generalize that which occurs to us so that we can prove our ego's need to be right, in other words, what we have learned and been conditioned by in the past still holds true in the present and future.

As humans, we sometimes have a tendency toward hasty generalization. This is of course, one of the logical fallacies. To speak in absolute terms such as "all," "none," "always," "never," "everyone," "no one," is to discount or ignore the rest of reality. Do you really NEVER catch a break? Does NOTHING ever change? When we focus on negative generalizations, we reduce our mental and spiritual awareness of the good things that are happening around us and to us every day.

Oddly enough, we stay in this space because it is comfortable. It is all we think that we know due to our past experiences and conditioning. Our ego is our small self; it is a false self. The ego is resistant to change because its frame of reference is always based on the past. The past is all it knows.

While we can improve our life by making positive changes to it, the factor of the unknown that comes with breaking out of our comfort zone creates fear, which always comes from the small ego. Its job is to keep us safe while helping us to understand the world. It finds reasons to keep us where we are, whether we are happy or not, because the small ego bases its decisions on that which is familiar.

Let us look at this more closely.

*Is **the world** truly against you, or are you just being melodramatic? Do you find that **no one** ever supports your decisions or that you are **always** are shot down when you propose a change?*

I doubt it.

These over-generalizations are illogical fallacies based on mistaken perceptions. They are easy to fall into, but are also easily countered by a small amount of investigation.

For example, let's assume that you have a belief that you can **never** win or that you **always** lose (you may substitute your own belief here). Take a moment to think about an example of when you did succeed, when you did the opposite of what you were being told by those around you (perhaps co-workers, family or friends). How did you feel in that moment of success? How do you feel by just remembering it?

These moments can be major or minor. The most basic, simplistic moment will work to prove this point.

Take, for example, the first time you walked without falling, the first time you cooked without burning your food, or perhaps the first time you landed a job. It does not matter how large or small the moment may have been, it only matters that these events took place and that you are now aware of them. Every moment makes an impression.

Some are greater than others due to trauma or a great deal of emotional involvement, and/or extreme conditioning.

Being aware of these times of achievement will help you to remember and/or learn something about yourself: You are capable of success. You have won in the past and you can win again.

At first, finding these moments may be difficult because we are not wired to see them. We are wired to see where we are deficient. We focus on what others have, are like, and have accomplished against that which we wish to have, be like or accomplish. What we see in the comparison is what we define as our failures.

To begin to see our successes, we must first be open to seeing them. We must learn to appreciate and show gratitude for the good things in our lives.

For example, maybe you have a job that is not earning you enough to pay your bills. You could look at the lack, at how you are falling behind financially. Or, you could look at the fact that you are holding your own. You are not losing as much money as you would if you did not have this job. It may not be an ideal situation, but it is where you are at this moment.

From the realization of where you are now, that in this moment you are safe, maybe you see that you now have 4 or 6 months of time to create a new future rather than facing the choice of staying in a job that causes so much stress.

My point here is not to tell you to be happy with a job that is not paying you enough; I am making this point to help you realize something that you can use to improve your life. Realize the lesson through gracious appreciation.

Then you can move forward with clarity, focusing on the positive things in your life.

By recognizing even just one of these moments, you have shattered the negative self-talk of "never" winning / "always" losing. ➤

At this point, your ego may still want to focus on 99% never winning/always losing.

That voice will sound something like, "Yeah, but..." *Ignore this voice.* Your power is in focusing on that percentage of winning, no matter how large or small. As you focus on even the smallest victories, you will know that you are capable of being successful.

This realization is the first step in breaking out of negative thought patterns and shifting your mindset toward success. You no longer need to fear failure.

When we stay locked in fear, we are feeding negative beliefs in ourselves that are rooted in our ego conditioning. Our ego wants us to stay in our comfort zone, living on decisions based in the past, on what is known. That is all that it knows and it feels safe in that space. To maintain that feeling of safety, it keeps us from taking risks to achieve our goals. Ego conditioning makes us believe that any changes can only have negative consequences.

Consider all the wealth created in the past decade; all of the new products and new companies that have become household words. Can you honestly say, "There is no more opportunity in the world" when you consider the sheer abundance of opportunity coming from just the Internet alone? When we focus on lack, we have no hope, we do not hear the guiding voice, we feel something is missing in our lives; but when we begin to focus on opportunity, we find avenues to advance our dreams.

MOVING TOWARD OPPORTUNITY

Now take a moment to focus on your dreams, the things you wish to accomplish, the goals that you have for yourself; the possibilities that you imagine. This could be the voice of your True Nature/True Self calling to you.

How can you tell whether it is the small ego or your True Self?

If this voice is pointing out your short comings and insurmountable obstacles, then it is not your True Self, it is the voice of the small ego.

Our ego is our false self; it is filled with conditioned responses, thoughts, emotions and behaviors. It consists of a personalized perception of emotions and thoughts wrought out from experiences "outside in the material world". It is the false self, mired in day-to-day living, the false self, stressed out over the bills that are due today/tomorrow/yesterday; the false self that focuses on what we think we cannot do. It is materialism and the focus on everything external and temporary rather than the pleasure of creating something that resonates with a higher perspective, purpose and goal.

Ego conditioning tells us to fear. It tells us that we are not good enough. It also tends to tell us that we will only be happy if certain outside circumstances occur. Have you ever said to yourself, "I'll be happy when _____ happens? I'll be happy when I am out of debt, I'll be happy when I have a new job or I'll be happy when I lose weight" ... the list goes on, and on, and on. The ego-self is defined as *conditioned consciousness that focuses on the negative aspects of life because it is based in fear.* It is the repetition of past thoughts and emotions triggered by situations, people, and things that we come across in the journey of life. It is a learned behavior and mindset as we watched others while we grew up. Anxiety is created when we project these thoughts and emotions of fear into the future. We believe that we all need to worry most of the time about most everything because "that could happen again and it was bad." Then we try to control what is outside of ourselves so that we may feel safe. That does not work. Therefore, we continue the same attitudes, wants and needs and the same behaviors, continually experiencing the same old, bad things over and over again. These are our perceptions about the world.

External validations of happiness are fleeting. As anyone who has ever looked forward to a new job after toiling in vain knows, the stress of an old job is usually repeated at the new location, because we take our ego sense-of-self with us wherever we go.

Right or wrong, we are what we think or feel about "ourselves." As we look to external, fleeting validation for our sense of worth, we are disappointed as we realize those things are temporary and eventually leave our lives. When a particular external validation is gone, we look for the next thing outside in the world that makes us feel good; and so it goes.

Only when we begin to connect with our higher perceptions, our True Self, can we realize our true nature as eternal beings. From this connection comes bliss and contentment. From this place of lasting happiness, we can manifest our purpose on this earth and realize true abundance and happiness that is not fleeting.

There is a voice in the back of our mind saying that we can do better than a paycheck-to-paycheck existence. It can guide us and show us how we can serve humanity rather than just accumulating for ourselves. It focuses on our purpose and goals and shows us how to work toward fulfilling our purpose. It tells us we are better than we currently believe.

This is the voice of our True Self which we do not hear or listen to most of the time. It lets us know that everything is and always will be OK as long as we accept what it tells us, shows us and guides us toward.

It will help us heal by showing us how to become aware of the false self and to release the emotions, thoughts, beliefs, and all the conditioning that hurts us, which stops us from fully being who we truly are.

It reminds us to be happy with what is NOW because our outlook is our choice. When we choose to be happy without ties to temporary, outside circumstances, then we begin to revolutionize our life. Then we do not live in the fear of loss or change. Instead we begin to actualize ourselves as the prosperous, joyful, passionate soul we were born to express.

We now can trust another part of ourselves. We now can start connecting with our "better selves," our souls – our True Selves. By doing this, we elevate our energy vibrations to a more spiritual level and begin attracting to ourselves more things that reinforce an experience of true happiness and greater abundance. We will discuss the Law of Attraction in Chapter 5.

There are the things that you specifically are here on this earth to experience and share. You have a purpose that is meant just for you to realize and accomplish. If you clear your mind and contemplate your goals, you can sense, on a physical level, if these goals are part of your path in this life or merely things that you "want" from an ego's perspective.

There are a number of questions we can ask ourselves to sense if our goals are coming from ego or our True Self. These questions include:

Do these goals bring joy to you? If you do the work necessary to make this goal a reality, is it work that you enjoy? Will it bring you satisfaction and a sense of accomplishment and peace?

Do these goals bring peace and happiness to others? Does the actualization of your goal help others; does it make the world a better place, no matter to what degree?

Do these goals move the world forward? Does your goal bring something to humanity that takes humanity forward? Does your goal bring relief and protection to endangered species? If just one person or one animal is helped by your goal, you can answer "yes" to this question.

To see if your goal is coming from ego, ask yourself this question:

Is the end result of these goals a transient, temporary satisfaction or creation? Will it disappear after your death or continue to live on as an idea or thing that will inspire others? If your goal benefits only you, then it is probably generating from ego.

If your goal is based upon the concept of limited resources, then it is generating from fear and therefore your ego self. For example, when you think about your goal, do you feel like you have to get there first because someone may "beat you to it?" Are you trying to protect "your piece of the pie" because there is not enough to share?

These are thoughts that are based in scarcity, lack and fear of not ever having enough. They are based in our ego conditioning. When we begin to align with our True Self, we see that abundance comes to us in many ways. We are no longer concerned with a lack of resources because we know that there is more than enough for everyone.

If you choose to do so, you can build a legacy that lives on after you which is for the greater good. These are the goals that are in balance with our life's purpose and the calling of our True Self.

OUR NEGATIVE INNER VOICES

The voice that just screamed, "This is bullshit!" in your head is your ego, the sum of your experiences formed of emotions and thoughts on this planet telling you that reality kills dreams and you need to just keep your nose down and work hard. You have already done that, and you probably never got very far.

I'll bet that voice sounded a lot like the one that tells you the limiting thoughts that you read a few paragraphs ago.

These voices tend to be loud. They also tend to sound a lot like our parents or critical friends/family members that we knew at a younger age. They have been with us for a long time, so we tend to listen to them over the voice of our True Self or images of our higher visions and dreams. Initially, ego emotions and thoughts are created by the voices of others. At some point in our lives, they may have actually been beneficial in keeping us out of trouble, but now, if they are getting in the way of our growth, healing and realization of our dreams, then these negative thoughts have to be released.

The process to quiet these voices is challenging. It requires deep introspection and self-evaluation. In my hypnotherapy practice, I use advanced techniques to help my clients heal and reframe these voices and the events that led to their creation.

To achieve our goals, we must find out why we want to reach them and also create a deeper understanding of ourselves. Outer and inner negative influences must be quieted or transformed into positive cheerleaders who rally us on rather than condemn our trying.

CHAPTER 1: Why Setting An Intention
Is Critical To Your Success

This is the most important chapter in changing your life. Your intention for your life is a powerful tool to keep you motivated and focused.

To make our goals lasting, we must fully understand why we want to change.

What is the big picture for your new life?

Why do you want to manifest your goal?

What intention do you have for making it happen?

Intention is our "Why." It keeps us on track when the path gets slow and muddy; when diversions and perceived setbacks distract us from the larger picture. Without a focus on our intent, we can get caught up in the details and slow down our process of manifestation. We become tactical instead of strategic.

What is the difference? A strategic approach to a problem looks at the larger scope – where we ultimately want to be, what we want to accomplish. A tactical approach takes us down into the details of how, when, where and with whom we achieve our goal.

Worrying about and focusing on these details will typically trap us in day-to-day thinking that does not help us in achieving our goal. What if the person you are working with, who you see as an intrinsic part of your dream, declines to participate? Now, instead of moving ahead focused on your large goal, you are stuck trying to figure out how to move ahead without this person.

Focusing on the large goal makes tactics less important. What really matters most is that we keep moving ahead toward that goal, not how every step is precisely placed.

Another way to look at manifesting goals is to use the metaphor of painting. If one is offered in your area, take part in a wine and art class one evening. Most areas of the country have small groups that offer these chances to paint while sampling wines and experiencing the creation of art.

If you have never painted before, you will find it to be an interesting experience. The teacher will hold up a sample painting. This is the image that all the students will work on recreating that evening.

This is, as Stephen Covey would call it in *The Seven Habits of Highly Effective People,* "Begin with the End in Mind." You see where you are going and you will begin your path to completion.

The next step is filling your canvas with broad strokes of color. Details and placement are not overly important for the most part, particularly in the early stages of creating your masterpiece.

What is significant is that you are doing the broad strokes that create the foundation for your art.

As the evening wears on, you will slowly add increasingly minor details. The specifics of the painting, the things that most people focus on when looking at a piece of art, are the final points to be added.

What does this have to do with manifesting your dream?

Everything!

When we examine art, we tend to focus on the final picture, particularly all the details and not focus on the process of broad strokes that comprise the majority of the image. Doing this separates us from the process of creating because we only let ourselves see the end result.

The big lesson here is to not be attached to details of outcomes. Allow yourself to see your goal in broad brushstrokes as you dream it. Allow the details to fill in as you move forward and you begin to make your goal real.

You may find that a detail that you painted earlier in the process is now out of place as your painting begins to take shape. You either choose to leave it or you paint over it, changing the landscape and revising your image as you work towards the outcome.

Set a plan in place that will take you to your goal. See smaller, achievable benchmarks along the way. These reference points will do two things: They will keep you on your path and they will keep you motivated as you see successes that build toward your goal.

To use a different metaphor, if your goal is to drive from New York to Los Angeles along the most efficient route, you would open a map (or use a GPS system). As you look at the driving path, you will mark milestones at each major city. When you arrive at one as you drive, you will know that you are that much closer to arriving at your destination.

However, without a clearly set goal regarding your route, you may suddenly find yourself in Toronto. Since you did not know exactly where you were heading, or you left without a clear intention for arriving in a certain amount of time or efficiency of miles driven, there's a good chance that you wasted a lot of effort.

Much like setting goals, nothing is ever final; each "crossroad" or step is merely a part in the process of continued achievement. As we move from our original starting point and we begin to achieve the smaller benchmarks that lead us to the outcome, we change. Our outlook changes as we experience success; our goals may change as we realize that our ultimate outcome is not quite what we truly wanted. Or, maybe we discover a new road that gets us to our goal more efficiently; the possibility also exists that we take a more difficult path, learning many different things than we would not have experienced otherwise, but we still arrive at the desired outcome.

At this point, it is critical that we give ourselves permission to re-evaluate our goals and/or change our paths.

Why continue moving toward a goal that is not ultimately fulfilling? …because you went to school for 4, 6 or 8 years to learn that occupation? …because it is the job your parent(s) did?

Trust yourself to make the right choice for your life.

How do you know which is the right choice is for you? It requires some work.

Ask yourself, "Why do I get out of bed in the morning?"

When you answer this, your response should not be "Because I have to go to work." There is more to that answer. Even if you do not enjoy your job, there is a reason beyond just a paycheck, that causes you to rise from sleep, prepare for the day and go to work. What is it? What aspects of your job bring you joy?

As I asked myself this question years ago, I ultimately discovered that I have a passion for problem solving and helping others.

This answer did not come to me overnight. It required weeks of deep questioning and self-introspection. Do not blindly accept the first answer that comes to you. Test it, see if it truly fits in with your larger goals and if it resonates as something you are passionate about.

Other questions to ask yourself:

What truly makes me happy?

Why do I care about _____? (insert topic, person, idea that draws your attention)

When do I feel happiest or most engaged with myself and/or others?

What do I want to accomplish in my life? What legacy do I want to leave?

How do I want to live my life so that I can be happy and realize my goals?

I suggest investing in Dr. Isaiah Hankel's book, *Black Hole Focus*. It is an excellent source of guidance for helping you to find what you are passionate about in life.

Once you know your intention for your life, begin fashioning goals that will help you to live in your intended way.

Choose large goals for yourself. Do not underestimate your power.

Chart your course with smaller benchmarks on your path toward success. Much like the cities in our GPS example above, these benchmarks will let you know that you are on-track.

Decide what is best for you – stay on your path. I promise you that it almost certainly will not be easy, but you will succeed.

The critical step here is that you must FULLY IMAGINE, SEE and FEEL yourself in that future success. This is where we engage our Reticular Activating System (RAS).

Have you ever noticed that when you are really down, nothing, and I mean NOTHING ever seems to go right? You just keep saying, "If I could just get one lucky break, I'd be in great shape." But that break never comes. You just continue to wallow in that space or begin a downward spiral until you hit rock-bottom.

Yet, I am sure you have friends for whom everything seems to always go right. They are happy, get all the lucky breaks and just keep moving forward with all of their dreams.

Do you know why? Because they believe they deserve those good things. They see the world as their oyster. They were happy because they accepted what was, then the good things started to happen – they attracted to themselves the things they desired through their acceptance and thoughts of abundance.

You can do the same thing.

Choose right now, right this moment, no excuses …give yourself a chance at a new life. To do that, you have to make some agreements:

1)   Release self-pity and victimhood. The only thing you are a victim to is your own outlook on the world.

2)   Release beliefs that there is such a thing as "bad luck" and that you there are "no breaks". By focusing on this negativity, you are attracting more of it to your life. (If you have difficulty breaking free of these negative beliefs, I suggest picking up a copy of *The Five-Minute Journal.* It will help you on your path, which leads directly to #3.)

3)   Focus on gratitude for what you already have. See the abundance in your life, no matter how small or seemingly insignificant it is to you, find positive things in your life and thank the Universe for them. Not sure where to start, try this: You are alive and reading this book. You have an innate knowledge that your life can be better and you are taking action. **You can do this!**

4)   Choose to move past your fears. They will come up as you move out of your comfort zone. When they arise, ask yourself, "Why am I afraid of this? What do I really have to lose by taking this chance? I know and trust that God/The Universe has my back."

Read and sign this page to show your commitment to your future as a co-creator in your life.

I, _____, promise to myself, on this date, _____, that I will choose to live my life with a positive purpose and mindset. I take responsibility for my choices and actions. I am moving forward knowing that my dream is entirely possible and I send it out into the Universe of Pure Potentiality to return to me as the Universe sees fit.

I understand that I must let go of attachment to the outcome. My dream may come back to me looking differently than I envisioned, but I recognize that this is how the Universe intends it to be and it is in accord with my highest Divine purpose.

I now set the intention for my life to become: _____

_____

_____.

Signature: _____

Date: _____

Exercise: Create a vision board

Vision boarding, also known as treasure mapping, has been used for years to help individuals consider what they want to bring to their future. It is a simple process and quite powerful.

To create your vision board, you will need a few things:

1.   Poster-board or cardboard that can be used as your base. The size does not matter, use the dimensions that feel right to you.

2.   Magazines that you can cut apart. It's best to have a variety available so that you can pick from a wide range of photos and words.

3.   Scissors and a glue stick.

Find a time to do this exercise when you can focus completely on your goals for your life. Some Unity or Science of Mind churches offer a vision boarding class. This is a fun, interactive way to bounce ideas off others and is actually an inspirational process. When we interact with like-minded individuals, we can bring out the best in each other.

I created my vision board at one of these classes at Unity Naples in Naples, Florida. The amount of joy within the room was incredible – everyone was asking about each other's goals and pulling pictures for each other. It was an experience of collective consciousness, so many individuals working on individual goals together.

As you begin building your vision board, look for pictures that resonate with and represent your dreams, your "ideal life." If your ideal car is a Porsche, do not paste a picture of a rusty pickup truck on your board, find a picture of a Porsche – the exact model you desire.

Look for headlines or type that state your goals, such as "New York Times Bestselling Author" or "Earn $1,000,000."

Once completed, place your board in an area where you will see it every day. Look at it with intention and let the images and words sink into your mind.

Exercise: Setting Intent Visualization

Visualization for Setting Intention

Sit in a comfortable chair with eyes closed. Focus on your breathing. Feel your diaphragm go up and down with every breath. Relax and allow yourself to go deeper within yourself as you continue breathing; do this until you feel you have settled in a quiet and still place within yourself.

First visualize your life as it is. Now visualize your fears and the negative thoughts being played out about why your goal/accomplishment cannot be realized. See what obstacles are in the way of your realizing your intended goal/accomplishment. Visualize solutions to remove these obstacles. If you need money, see the money coming to you, do not worry about where the money is coming from or the why, how or when the money will arrive. See yourself holding the money; see the money flowing to you. You are connecting with supportive energies that will help you to manifest your goal/accomplishment.

Then visualize a time in your past when you were faced with a challenge. Any challenge at all. Remember how you overcame that obstacle, realize that you were successful then as you opened to the possibilities available to you to solve the problem. You manifested the solution to realize your success. Once again feel the power that you felt in that moment.

Allow yourself to be in that moment of power. Once again, feel how you felt as you moved past those temporary fears and negative thoughts and know that all blockages are temporary. Know now, in this moment, that you can repeat this success at any time, including realizing your current goal.

Realize that your goals and dreams are just beyond your fears due to the unknown. Let go of the control that these fearful thoughts have over you. Remember that these negative beliefs which were generated from the past have nothing to do with the now or the future.

As you once again feel the power of your past success, carry it forward with you to this present moment.

Now visualize how you will help others through manifesting your intent. Realize any impure or improper reasons for desiring this goal/accomplishment. If it is ego conditioning such as: "I want to be rich." "I want others to envy me." "I want to be a superstar."; there is no true power of creative force behind it, as ego conditioning is low vibrational energy due to self-gratifying emotions and thoughts such as greed, feeling of power, lust, and so on. When you hold compassion and love in your heart for others and know that what you manifest will help not only yourself but many people, you are backed by the very high vibrational energy of the creative force. "I want to heal others through my accomplishments; to help them to better themselves or their lives." "I wish others to be free of pain and misery."

Visualize your intent as fully as possible. See your goal/accomplishment as if you are living it now. Connect with your passion, the enthusiasm towards living this which you intended, apply the power of the action to further the goal/accomplishment and feel great gratitude and give thanks for this coming to be. Continue to hold compassion and love in your heart for others. See how you are helping them through the realization of your goal/accomplishment. Then feel their gratitude towards you, their love and acceptance of what you have accomplished for yourself and them.

Stay in the quiet, still place within you until you know that your intent has been set within you.

Then focus on your breathing again and take one or two deep cleansing breaths and open your eyes.

Live everyday like you are on your way to realizing what is destined to be; that is the manifestation of your goal/accomplishment.

CHAPTER 2: How Do Affirmations
Affect Manifestation?

What does it mean to affirm something? What are affirmations? More importantly, why is it important to understand these distinctions?

According to Merriam Webster:

Affirm: (v) (1) to say that something is true in a confident way; (2) to show a strong belief in or dedication to (something such as an important idea)

Affirmation: (n) the act of affirming; something affirmed: a positive assertion; an act of saying or showing that something is true

Affirmations seem like easy things to write and use, but why do so many people have trouble with them? People see limited results (or no results at all) and give up after only a few days of recitation.

One reason may be that they are using affirmations that are not worded in a way that resonates with their primary method of interaction with the world. We will explore this idea in a moment.

Another reason may be that they are wording their affirmations incorrectly. This is a very common mistake. It is also one that is easily corrected to create powerful tools for you to achieve your goals.

Imagine you are going on a diet. You have a goal of eating healthfully and avoiding sweets like cake and cookies. To help you with your goal, you write the following affirmation to say daily:

"I will not eat cake."

Easy, right?

What is the first thing that came to mind after you read that sentence? What word stood out to you the most?

It was probably "cake," and now you are hungry for a piece. You are now focused on desiring exactly the thing that you are telling yourself not to want. Why?

When we're talking about our goals, our subconscious mind tends to ignore the word "not." Instead, it focuses attention on that which we are thinking about in our conscious mind. The last thing that we present is what tends to stay in focus.

Whatever is present in our thoughts is what we bring creative force to; it is what we manifest in our lives. How does this apply to the example above?

Rather than hearing "I will not eat cake," your subconscious heard, "I will eat cake," possibly even just the key words, "eat cake."

This same principle applies to other goals that we attempt to manifest for ourselves.

Our subconscious mind is the place where we hold our repressed emotions and beliefs about ourselves. It is also the seat of our creativity and the control room for our autonomic bodily functions.

In fact, we could consider our subconscious as our connection to our higher awareness or to the collective unconsciousness.

From this perspective, our subconscious is in direct contact with The Universal Mind, God Consciousness. A bit later in this book, we will dissect Matthew 7:7-11: "Ask and you shall receive, seek and you shall find, knock and the door will be open to you."

For now, let us just examine this Bible quotation at face value.

This quote from the Bible brings to awareness that your soul, your subconscious mind, is able to converse with The Universal Mind in order to co-create your life. First, the blockage of beliefs, emotions and repetitive thoughts must be removed to allow co-creating to occur. The negative mindset to which you have become conditioned will be the driving force of your life if it is not dealt with. The soul subconscious waits patiently to be heard, but cannot and will not *strong arm* the conditioned mindset out of the way, because you have the choice to turn towards ego conditioned chatter or not. How do you deal with the deeply rooted ego-driven conditions within the soul subconscious? Meditation, therapy, mindfulness practice and other modalities allow you to go inward and root out the negatively conditioned mindset.

The deeper you go, the more you connect with soul (which is your True Self and part of your Higher Self – the I Am; the All-Knowing, All-Seeing part of the Soul). The Higher Self is the highest consciousness that you are able to access. Your True Self is co-creator with your Higher Self. We will discuss this concept more deeply in the *What is Creator?* section in chapter 4.

If you want to be wealthy, writing "I will not be poor," or "I no longer have financial troubles" will keep you trapped in a world of debt and money fears because you are focused on lack rather than abundance.

If you want to exercise every day to become healthy, lean and muscular, writing "I don't want to be fat" will guarantee that you will continue to be sedentary rather than active.

As you review the examples above, what stands out to you? What common thread runs through each of the affirmations?

Answer: They are written in the negative and each is *focused on the thing that we do not want.*

Instead of healthy foods, the first example focuses on cake; instead of wealth and abundance, the second example focuses on poverty/financial troubles; and the third focuses on fat instead of fit.

What each of these affirmations does is affirm that which we do not want. They bring the thing we are trying to avoid or change directly into our awareness and our Reticular Activating System (RAS). We will discuss the RAS in depth in the next chapter.

As I stated earlier, another possible issue with ineffective affirmations is that they are written in a way that does not resonate with how you perceive and interact with the world.

All of us interact with the world around us in one of three ways: visually, kinesthetically or auditorily. What does this mean and how do we find out our method? More importantly, why does it matter?

It matters because as we begin to meditate and imagine ourselves realizing our goals, the affirmations that you create should be written in the language of your method of interaction.

If you relate to the world in a visual way, you probably tend to say things like, "I see where you're coming from," or "Paint a picture for me." The terms used are centered on sight or visual input.

A kinesthetic person would say things like, "Let's touch on this during our discussion," or "I'm not feeling warm and fuzzy about this." The terms used tend to relate to physical interactions.

An auditory person utilizes, you guessed it, sound cues: "I hear what you are saying," "That sounds good to me."

We all relate to the world primarily in one of these three methods. Sometimes we use two or all three to varying degrees, but one will always be our primary method.

Let us find your primary method.

Read the next paragraph, then relax, close your eyes, take a deep breath and allow yourself to experience your imagination.

Imagine yourself at the beach. The sun is in the sky above you, the sand extends out to the sea and far off to your left and right. There are others with you at the beach today: families, friends, small groups having fun in the sand and surf. Seagulls fly overhead. Step to the water's edge as the waves gently roll in and out.

Now close your eyes and take a deep breath and imagine yourself in that scene. Let it fill your senses for a few seconds. Relax. I will be here when you get back.

    * * *

Welcome back! How was your trip to the beach?

As you recall your visit, what comes to mind?

Did you see yourself standing on the sand, people all around you? Did you see the sunlight shining off the water, a variety of colors of skins and bathing suits? Did you see the gulls in the sky?

Or maybe you felt the warmth of the sand on your body? Did you feel the closeness of the other people? Did you sense the heat of the sun or the **coolness** of the water; maybe you felt a breeze blow in from the sea?

Or did you hear the surf? Perhaps as gentle washes or rolling or as crashing waves? Did you hear the other people laughing or screaming in joy? Maybe their radios were playing. How did the gulls sound as they called out to each other in the sky?

Which of these descriptions best recalls your experience? Maybe you experienced two different reactions at the same time. If so, which one creates more presence for you? If you saw the scene but also felt the sand/sun/water, does one of those experiences seem to be more immediate, more complete?

As you have probably already figured out, if you saw the beach, noticed sunlight reflecting off the waves as they rolled into the shore as you pictured gulls flying overhead, you interact with the world in a visual way. If you felt the sand under your feet, sensed the salty air of the ocean and felt the warm sun on your skin, your method of interaction is kinesthetic. If you heard the waves rolling or crashing into the shore, listened to the gulls calling overhead and the ocean breeze whispered in your ear, you are an auditory person.

Make a note here of your primary method.

"I relate to the world primarily in a_____
manner."

As we move forward, keep your primary method in mind. When we write affirmations and perform meditations, use the words that best describe your sensations. I am primarily a visual person, so I tend to write my affirmation as "I now see myself as a healthy, vibrant person."

If you are primarily a kinesthetic person, write your affirmations using touch references such as, "I now feel happy and healthy," "My goals are now within my grasp."

As an auditory person, your affirmations will be something like, "I hear my higher calling and follow it," "I am in harmony with my highest intention. I listen for my guidance."

Here is a small list of words for each method of interaction that you can use when writing your own affirmations.

VISUAL	KINESTHETIC	AUDITORY
See	Feel	Hear
Picture	Sense	Sound
Bright/Dark	Hot/Warm/Cool/Cold	Loud/Quiet
Colorful	Smooth/Sharp	Tone (i.e. I don't like the
Painted	Texture(s)	tone of your voice...)
Look	Grasp	Harmony
Clear	Get a grip	Silence
Focused	Get a handle on	Listen
View	Tap into	Ring (i.e. That rings
Visualize	Reach out	true...)
		Voice (i.e. Voice your
		opinion...)

CHAPTER 3: Grounding and Centering:
Why You Must Start With Balanced Energy

As we work our way through this book and realize how we can transform our lives, we will be releasing the past and healing ourselves through meditations and visualizations. One of the most important steps to beginning this journey is for you to be grounded.

Without grounding to this plane and connecting with the Earth, it becomes easy for us to just fly off into ego ideas and not bring them down to the practical level of life. Instead of implementing our goals, we may just think about them and feel good.

Meditation is a key step to quieting our conscious mind, removing the noise and distractions around us so that we can focus on higher thoughts and goals. Being drawn into the dramas of family, friends and celebrities or the trivial consequences of sports will just keep you mired in the short-term. You will be robbing yourself of your large goals; you will only see anthills and you will miss the majestic mountains that are full of life around you.

Why Meditate – Benefits of Meditation

Meditation allows the flow of energy or universal life force to more easily enter your body. It helps heal and alter the mind and body, permitting a "holistic" outcome. Eventually, it can affect healthy change at the molecular level.

On a physical level, the benefits of meditation are many. It helps:

- Lower blood pressure
- Decrease tension which causes tension headaches, ulcers, insomnia, muscle and joint problems and other stress-induced illnesses
- Balance melatonin and serotonin levels that improves mood and behavior and allows you to rest and relax
- Improve the immune system
- Energy or vitality is increased
- On the psychological level, meditation helps:

- Change brainwave activity to the Alpha state which allows for higher brain function to occur, thereby increasing rational thinking and behavior, clarity and focus.
- Anxiety decreases
- Emotional stability improves
- Creativity increases
- Happiness increases
- Intuition develops
- Peace of mind flows
- Provide an expanded consciousness/awareness
- On the emotional level, meditation helps:
- Emotional steadiness and harmony
- Feel less overwhelmed
- More stable emotionally – less moody, fewer or no outbursts of raw emotion
- Emotionally available – know what you are feeling
- Have control over emotions, as opposed to the other way around

Meditation Brings Harmony in Creation

Meditation **assists** you to find within yourself the vastness of space, calmness and joy. You are able to connect with your higher brain function in the middle to upper parts of the brain. The lower part of the brain - the "reptilian brain" associated with fear and emotion - is involved in the initiation of the body's response to stress, "fight or flight." It is reactive. We will discuss this part of the brain in depth in Chapter 8.

Meditation helps to re-wire the neural pathways to higher brain function in the pre-frontal cortex which is associated with awareness, concentration and decision-making. Without getting into too much scientific explanation, it has been proven through many research studies over approximately 30 years that meditation is beneficial in many ways.

At the University of Massachusetts Medical School, Jon Kabat-Zinn, Ph. D., studied the effects of meditation on a group of employees from a high-tech company in Wisconsin. The total number of participants was 41; 25 were asked to learn meditation over an eight-week course, the other 16 were not given mediation assignments and were considered the control group.

The brainwaves of all participants were scanned as part of the study. Those in the meditation group showed signs of being calmer and happier than before the study.

According to tmhome.com, a website dedicated to Transcendental Meditation, the positive effects of meditation can be seen with just a small-time commitment: "if practiced regularly, 2 times 20 minutes per day — will open up your intellectual and cognitive capacities."

Meditation can help us to hear our positive inner voices. When we take the time to quiet outside noise and focus on our goals, we begin to discover connections and open to our True and Higher Selves. As we become calmer and happier through meditation, the noise in our heads and around us lessens. We become less distracted by transitory problems that used to capture our attention. We begin to focus on our growth and our goals; we can achieve greater clarity.

Clear thinking helps to realize a "better new self" and a better environment to live in "out there," creating a harmonious and happy outlook on life which helps you attract what you need in order to create a better life.

We will discuss the Law of Attraction in Chapter 5.

Personal Transformation

Meditation can bring about a true personal transformation. As the brain is re-wired, we learn more about ourselves mentally and emotionally. We start to heal, letting go of out-worn beliefs and knowledge that was learned in the past.

The past should be left there, in the past; much of what was learned long ago does not apply to the present or to the future. We hopefully learned our lessons so that we could move forward, not so we could be mired in the past for the rest of our lives. Higher brain function allows us to see this and help to make transformation an easier experience. As we become healthier and happier individuals, we attract what we are searching for much easier, connecting with our higher awareness and allowing the flow of manifesting to happen without much effort.

Preparation

Find a room or some space in your home, office or studio where you will be undisturbed. If you like and are able, you may want to use a lighted candle, some fresh flowers and some lighted incense, to help create a calming atmosphere or aromatherapy oils can be used to purify the space. You may wish to play some gentle flute music or some type of sounds such as ocean waves in the background to help you focus on the meditation allowing thoughts to flow through your mind unnoticed more easily. Make sure you will be warm and comfortable and that it is as quiet as possible; switching off cell phones, etc. Placing a shawl, or blanket around your shoulders or lap may be a wise thing to do; it is common while meditating to feel cooler. Wear loose, comfortable clothing. Try preparing yourself for meditation the same way each time you decide to sit in meditation. This will enable you to become focused and relaxed more quickly and easily as your mind will create a habit to do so, thereby making meditation "more pleasant and easier to do."

Postures

There are two comfortable choices regarding posture. Sit upright in a chair with your feet flat on the floor. It is preferable to sit for meditation keeping your back straight. Or you may choose to sit on a cushion on the floor. You can do this by sitting cross-legged choosing a cushion that elevates your buttocks. Rest your hands in your lap with your right hand nestled in the palm of your left hand with thumbs slightly touching at the tips or on your lap, open palms up or down.

The first meditation will be one of grounding.

Over the next few pages you will find two versions of "The Tree of Life Grounding Meditation." One version is spiritually-focused, while the other is for those where the wording of the spiritual version does not resonate. Either will be effective, use the version you feel most comfortable with.

This guided meditation will help to align you with the energies of the Universe and the Earth in order to get centered and grounded. A recording of this meditation is available at www.practicalmanifesting.com.

All things in the Universe have energy fields, as science has proven. A tree is part of a grid within a universal ecosystem. Envisioning yourself as a tree may help you understand how that system works and allows your connectivity to absorb the revitalizing and nurturing force of energy. Grounding allows higher vibrational energy to move through you without short-circuiting or over-loading your personal energy field.

Centering helps you to connect with what you are able to realize: feelings of togetherness, love, wholeness and so on. Also, grounding and centering before you sit for other types of meditation - such as healing, releasing and/or transcendental meditation - allows for better results.

Prepare yourself to sit in meditation. Close your eyes and relax. If you are not listening to the guided meditation online, envision the following:

Non-Spiritual version of The Tree of Life Grounding Meditation

Visualize yourself as a tree. Your feet and legs are healthy, strong roots, the trunk of your body is the trunk of your tree and your arms and hands are beautiful, large branches. Perhaps they hold fruit, lovely flowers or healthy green leaves. See your roots growing into the Earth. Through the grass or ground and ground water; through the clay and rock formations; through the minerals and crystals; through the heat and lava into the center of the Earth. In the center of the Earth is a huge, multi-faceted crystal full of different colored lights. It moves as if it is phasing in and out of the 3rd dimensional reality. It is full of energy, vibrating to the Earth's core force. Allow your roots to connect with this crystal. Feel/sense/hear/imagine the energy of the Earth. It is comforting, nurturing, revitalizing. You feel very connected to the Earth, grounded in its gravity. As you stay grounded, feel/sense/hear/imagine the comforting, nurturing, revitalizing energy move up your roots. It feels like cool water running up along your roots to nourish you and support your life and growth on the Earth. The energy moves up your roots through the heat and lava, through the minerals and crystals, up through the clay and rock formations through the water and ground into the trunk of your tree; Into its center, the heart. Feel/sense/hear/imagine the comforting, nurturing, revitalizing energy within you.

Now visualize your beautiful, strong branches. See them growing upward, higher and higher into the sky. They grow through the clouds, into the upper atmosphere. They grow toward the moon; higher and higher past the moon into outer space. Your branches grow through outer space past all the planets between here and the Sun, The Source. Allow your branches to grow into the Sun. Feel/sense/hear/imagine the fire burning, the light it emits, and the pull of the Sun bringing you to connect with the great power of creation within it, the strength and authority of this great power and the power of life. Feel/sense/hear/imagine this great power, the light and heat of The Source flowing down your branches through outer space past all the planets between here and the Sun. It flows down your branches toward and past the moon; then down your branches into the atmosphere of the Earth then into the trunk of your tree, into your heart. Feel/sense/hear/imagine the great power of Source, creation, within you; Its strength, authority and life itself bringing you what you need to co-create.

Feel/sense/hear/imagine the power of creation. The Sun/Source and the supporting, re-vitalizing energy of the Earth come together to bring balance and wholeness. You are centered and grounded. Stay connected to your heart.

Spiritual version of The Tree of Life Grounding Meditation

Visualize yourself as a tree. Your feet and legs are healthy, strong roots, the trunk of your body is the trunk of your tree and your arms and hands as beautiful large branches. Perhaps they hold fruit, lovely flowers or healthy green leaves. See your roots growing into the Earth. Through the grass or ground and ground water; through the clay and rock formations; through the minerals and crystals; through the heat and lava into the center of the Earth. In the center of the Earth is a huge, multi-faceted crystal full of different colored lights. It moves as if it is phasing in and out of the 3rd dimensional reality. It is full of energy, vibrating to the Earth's core force. This is the soul of the Mother of the Earth, Gaia. Allow your roots to connect with this Mother Earth's soul. Feel/sense/hear/imagine the energy of Gaia. It is loving and compassionate, comforting, nurturing, revitalizing. You feel very connected to Gaia, you know her; she is familiar to you. She is the Primal Mother. She provides all that you need to survive and experience life through a vessel, the physical body. As you stay grounded to the Earth, feel/sense/hear/imagine energy, love and compassion move up your roots. It feels like cool water running up along your roots to nourish you and support your life and growth on the Earth. The energy moves up your roots through the heat and lava, through the minerals and crystals, up through the clay and rock formations through the water and ground into the trunk of your tree, into its center your heart. Feel/sense/hear/imagine Gaia's love and compassion within you. It is comforting, nurturing, revitalizing.

Now visualize your beautiful, strong branches. See them growing upward, higher and higher into the sky. They grow through the clouds, into the upper atmosphere. They grow toward the moon; higher and higher past the moon into outer space. Your branches grow through outer space past all the planets between here and the Sun, Father Sky. Allow your branches to grow into Father Sky. Feel/sense/hear/imagine the fire burning, the light it emits, and the pull of Father Sky. It is the Primal Father. It also is very familiar. It is The Source bringing you to connecting with the great power of creation within it, the strength and authority of this great power and the power of life. Feel/sense/hear/imagine this great power, the light and heat of The Source flowing down your branches through outer space past all the planets between here and the Sun. It flows down your branches toward and past the moon; then down your branches into the atmosphere of the Earth then into the trunk of your tree, into your heart. Feel/sense/hear/imagine the great power of Source, creation, within you; Its strength, authority and life itself. It brings you what you need to co-create.

Feel/sense/hear/imagine the power of creation, strength and life, Father Sky, and the love, and compassion which is supporting, re-vitalizing energy of Mother Earth come together to bring balance and wholeness. You are centered and grounded. You are empowered now to co-create with Father Sky and are supported by Mother Earth to manifest that which you came to co-create in this physical plane of existence. Stay connected to your heart.

Repeat this meditation regularly to improve your connection to the Earth as you continue your journey through the manifesting process outlined throughout the rest of this book. Grounding is essential to maintaining your balance and being connected to the energies of manifestation.

After you perform this meditation daily for one week, you should gain an increased sense of peacefulness and calm in your life. Continue to perform this meditation to strengthen your connection to the Earth.

We'll move forward with creating your goals and the tools you will use to manifest them into reality.

CHAPTER 4: What Is The Relationship Between Creator, Co-Creator and You?

What is Creator?

You are creator!

As you will learn later in this book, you are also co-creator.

Creator is a person or thing that brings something into existence, for example an artist, writer, chef, musician or entrepreneur.

Religiously speaking and in the spiritual sense, it is considered The Universal Mind or pure consciousness in which Spirit (Existence) and Creator/God (awareness) are One. Described as Sat-Chit-Ananda in the Hindu Culture, it is the pure, undifferentiated state of non-duality. It is the most perfect expression of our primordial Self which is energetically inseparable from the power of Love (God) creating the Universe.

If you realize this state, you experience bliss, the essence of Life Itself and the Awareness of Awareness Itself (Pure Consciousness). You exist so it stands to reason that you are part of all existence; therefore, you are also part of The Universal Mind which can create anything, and has done so.

Sri Aurobindo a great East Indian master of the past stated, *"Everyone has in him something divine, something his own, a chance of perfection and strength in however small a sphere which God offers him to take or refuse. The task is to find it, develop it and use it. The chief aim of education should be to help the growing soul to draw out that in itself which is best and make it perfect for a noble use."*

Many have attested to this in such writings as diverse as the Bible, The Hermetic Principles, the Vedas, different gospels and scriptures from many cultures, personal teachings of the Buddha, of enlightened sages and those who in modern day have realized this truth. They have different names for this Universal Mind but, as was stated in the introduction, it is all the same one thing; one God known by many names.

The Universal Mind creates all of existence. You are part of this Mind. So, would it not make sense that your function is to create, not just in the physical sense, but in the higher sense as well?

"Mind over matter" is a truth. This is a phrase that has been used in several contexts in spiritual doctrines, parapsychology and philosophy. You have probably read stories about the placebo effect, where people are told they are being given a drug to address their condition or disease, but are actually given a sugar pill or another inert substitute. Some people achieve the healing goal of the drug from merely receiving the suggestion of the delivery of the drug, whether they took the drug or not. If the physical reaction of the medicine was not present to create the healing, what made it happen? The only possible answer is the person believed that it would happen, that they would heal.

Similar stories of "mind over matter" illustrate people overcoming extreme pain, lifting huge objects, such as cars, when in certain serious situations. At these moments, they are ignoring the perceived limitations of the self and just doing what needs to be done.

Quantum physics has proven that all matter at the subatomic level exists in wave form, and that matter only appears solid when we observe the wave. We use our senses to perceive the wave patterns in space and time. Thoughts form measurable wave patterns which have been proven to affect observable matter in the physical world.

In his book, *The Biology of Belief,* Dr. Bruce Lipton describes his journey from traditional, Western biology where matter interacting with matter on the physical level is the only source of healing (medicine brings about a physical change to the body), to a quantum/Eastern philosophy that recognizes the interaction of the mind and energy on healing (belief in change brings about a change in the body).

All this is not stated to persuade you; it is to inform you of the truth.

You are the creator of all that you experience physically, mentally, emotionally and even spiritually. As we have already discussed, through the choices you have made in this life, you have brought yourself to this exact moment, and these circumstances. No one else is responsible for your current state. Your choices in what to believe, in how to act or to react, and intentions manifest the experiences in your life, whether for the good or bad and whether you realize it or not.

This quote says it all, *"Life isn't about finding yourself. Life is about creating yourself."* — George Bernard Shaw.

How to Trust Creator

The Universal Mind has your back. Have faith.

You may be seeking It; that connection to something bigger than you. You may not be interested in it at all. Faith is still needed, not in The Creator or something bigger than us, but in *yourself.* This faith is in the power and abilities that you hold within; that *"...chance of perfection and strength... The task is to find it, develop it & use it..."* to *"...help the growing soul to draw out that in itself which is best and make it perfect for a noble use."* as stated in the quote from Sri Aurobindo earlier in this chapter.

Have faith that you are realizing your True Self and perhaps your Higher Self as you work on your ego conditioning. The flow of creating force will be available to you to develop and use for the greater good of The All. You are part of The All; therefore, wonderful things, abundance, happiness and so much more will be yours. This is where the Golden Rule applies.

From the New International Version (NIV) of the Bible: "So in everything, do to others what you would have them do to you, for this sums up the Law and the Prophets." Matthew 7:12

This is the Law of Pure Potential at work. Everything is available to you, everything can be manifested. Abundance is not lack; it is not fear of someone else getting there first. It is you being where you are at the proper time. As you open yourself to your higher awareness, you will see and feel your path more clearly and know that all is well as you do what needs to be done with keeping the greater good of all in mind.

Faith is needed because that which is most important will be done. Faith is trust. Faith shows the Universal Mind that you are trusting of It and that It works through you through your choices and actions. Faith is a higher energy vibration than ego. Faith gives us a tool to use consciously when the fears and negativity of our ego selves try to stop us from growing out of our comfort zones.

Faith gives us power over the physical realm.

That person who lifted that extremely heavy car did so not because they thought they could, but because they knew they had to save a person trapped beneath it. The sugar pill did the job because that person knew that they would heal and should heal. What is supposed to be will be done through you. *You are the soul through which that which is supposed to happen will be.*

This is in accordance with The Law of Cause and Effect.

This law is applicable to every human experience, situation and/or condition. Nothing is outside this law. Divine Will always works through cause and effect to correct and harmonize whatever is discordant by creating the "reap what you sow" scenario. There are other laws in effect here also, but the main force is this law.

In reality, the problem is ego-thought. It creates the disharmony and incorrect points-of-view which must be overcome. Tools for overcoming ego-thought include mindfulness of the present moment and a mindset of gratitude.

By focusing on appreciation of what is present and good in our lives, we learn to trust that all is well. As we move past the fears and negative perspectives of ego, which tend to replay the past and project the future, we learn to accept that we are OK in the present moment.

Becoming aware of the fears projected by ego conditioning is essential to growth. The past is over. We can no longer change it. Learn from it, yes, but those lessons must come without judgement.

The future is beyond our control. Setting goals is appropriate, worrying about every detail regarding their manifestation is not.

Projecting fear towards an outcome is also not appropriate. For example, worrying about if a person you are attracted to will reject your request for a date. This anticipation of a negative response is "ego talking," keeping you from potentially being hurt. But remember, the person could say yes. Accept the possibility of them saying no and embrace all of the possibilities present in the asking.

By accepting all possibilities, we place ourselves in the present. It's as if we are at a fork in a road with infinite options for our travels. Some roads may be pleasant, some may be challenging, some may be both (most are).

Fear can keep us at that junction. Faith that we will be OK, no matter which road we choose, allows us to move forward with confidence.

By embracing faith, we accept that no matter what happens to us, we are exactly where we are supposed to be at any given moment, making the choices we are supposed to make and, ideally, learning the lessons we are supposed to learn.

This type of faith creates a shift in the physical world allowing the Universal Mind to work through you. The axiom, "As above, so below; as below, so above" from *The Kybalion* speaks to this.

The intention and attention that is put out in the physical world will be supported by the Universe but that support may appear in different ways than expected.

That is why an attachment to an outcome of any type must be released. If you believe you know how something is to manifest, you block the flow of what may lead you to your highest good. We must wait and see what happens. For example, let us say that you would like to win a million dollars through the Lotto. But that never happens. You become aggravated and cannot understand why it is not coming to be; in your mind, you have done everything right to manifest this outcome.

However, you did not take into account that you had received an inheritance of $50,000 during the span of time you have been expecting a Lotto win. The inheritance was supposed to be, not the Lotto win. But this could be an obvious example.

Another example could be that you ask for your dream job to appear. You know what it is, obviously, you know what you are good at, the money you would like to make and roughly the type of work that you excel in and which you enjoy. Do you really know what you dream job should be? Do you really understand what you have come here to do in the physical world? Do you know your destiny? Through your manipulation of what you believe is right or true for you, you may eventually stop that which is supposed to be from actually happening.

This is a common blockage.

Many of us ignore anything other than that which we expect or want to happen and, therefore, miss the opportunity of finding our true dream job or calling because it does not fit into our limited criteria.

That is why healing mentally, emotionally and even physically is very important. It is to release that which could get in your way of receiving the higher energy of faith, in trusting the creator within you. Many wisdom traditions have told us that the source of creation is within ourselves because what is seen, felt, believed within is projected outwards.

To see yourself or tell yourself that you are a failure, you will project that in the physical world. Believe that you are successful and a winner and you will project that confidence in the world.

"Dear ones, we have created each other in our fantasy," a declaration by a sage found in the Vedanta, Eastern ancient scriptures. We all need to see through the illusion of what our fantasies have created and be willing to see the truth and trust it.

Creator is...

Consciousness. The Spiritual Laws following this chapter will explain further that everything is within The Universal Mind. We are part of this mind as we do, feel, think, experience and exist in It. There are different levels of consciousness based upon millions of different vibrations from highest to lowest. Science has proven this is how material objects are created through the energy vibrating forces within the objects making them appear solid or real. Therefore, if all is mind, then through changing the vibrations of your thoughts and emotions, you can release low vibrations of energy. If you are then able to vibrate at a higher level, you will connect with higher consciousness and thus connect with the true creator within.

But here is the big question: "Am I the Creator?" Yes and no. You are the co-creator in the physical world which is part of The Universal Mind, the source of creation where all possibilities lie and the power to manifest exists. You alone do not hold the power of creation. If you are able to surrender the ego self and the control over the outside world, the conditioned meddling will cease and the power of creation can flow unimpeded through you.

Miracles can happen.

How does Creator Work?

As The Universal Mind – God Consciousness is The Creator.

It is not for you to go seeking in the physical world for what you want manifested. That is your ego-self searching for what is only one thing in all the endless possibilities. Your ego self has only a limited perception of the abundance of possibilities available to you. Focusing on a single, or only a few, potential outcomes is not being open to the flow of abundance and the power of The Creator.

Manifesting is based on making a personal connection to the Infinite, to Pure Potential.

Seek inwardly to find your connection to The Creator through your I AM (Christ Consciousness/The Higher Self) for they are One.

What is God Consciousness and what is the I AM Consciousness?

The Vedanta often describes God as Sat-Chit-Ananda. Sat (Existence, Reality, Being), Chit (Consciousness, or Knowledge), and Ananda (Bliss). Existence, Consciousness and Bliss are not attributes of Brahman but Brahman Itself.

I AM is that portion of the Self that can translate to the individual soul some understanding of the perfections of God; Its Power, Its Knowledge.

I AM is that portion of your being that is real enough to stand in the Holy Presence of God to work as the Higher Mind, being that all-knowing and all-seeing Self of God, and that understands what is to be manifested. The I AM is One with God.

When utilizing prayer, meditation, contemplation or other ways of asking with humility and respect, only after you have purified the ego false self-conditioning well enough, will all that you deserve appear to you.

In the classic work, *John Gill's Exposition of the Entire Bible,* Gill dissects one of the most famous and frequently quoted phrases from the Bible: Matthew 7:7-11.

Ask and it shall be given you. *This is to be understood of asking of God in prayer, for such things as are wanting; whether of a temporal nature, as food and raiment, which Christ, in the former chapter, had warned against an immoderate and anxious concern for; or of a spiritual nature, as grace, and wisdom to behave in a proper manner, both toward God and men: and such, who ask according to the will of God, in the name of Christ, and under the* *direction, guidance, and influence of the Spirit, who ask in faith and fear, and with submission to the divine will, shall have what they ask for; not as what they deserve, but as a free gift.*

Seek, and ye shall find. *This is still meant of prayer, and of seeking God, his face and favour: which such shall find, who seek in a right way, by Christ, and with their whole hearts, diligently:* **knock and it shall be opened unto you as beggars do, who use much importunity for relief and assistance.** *So men should stand and knock at the door of mercy, which will not always be shut against them. Faith in prayer is a key that opens this door, when a poor soul finds grace and mercy to help it in time of need. Our Lord's design is to express the nature, fervour, and constancy of prayer, and to encourage to it.*

Prayer or meditation lead us to connection to our Higher Self. Acceptance of, and connection to something larger than our ego selves is crucial to manifesting.

Why?

Because, as we have already discussed, when we work just within the confines of our finite, ego-self, we have limited options. Only when we open to the Infinite, to Pure Potentiality, are then all things possible.

Christ Consciousness is your Higher Self, your I AM. It is the all-knowing, all-seeing super-soul self. As you realize your individual soul and it seeks connectivity to your Higher Self, you will be aligned with God Consciousness and Spirit: The Universal Mind. The hierarchy rises from Personal Soul Consciousness to Super-Soul Consciousness to God Consciousness, which is enlightenment.

If you have faith, the power to manifest will be yours, but you must hold gratitude and acceptance in your heart. Understand that all things out there are created by The Universal Mind and that you are within that Mind. It is important that you never try to cajole, control, or look in any other direction other than toward the I AM/God Consciousness. These attempts at control are coming from your ego; they come from our limited beliefs about ourselves and our place in the world; they come from our comfort zone.

The function or principle of God Consciousness and Spirit is to constantly create. You can co-create with It, as mentioned before, but you must accept that It does what It does for Its own reason, because that is what It does. This is another way of saying release your attachment to outcomes and allow The Flow to happen.

Your outcome may not be delivered to you in the way your ego-based desires dictate, but it will come to you in some form.

The Universal Mind is an impersonal force that, when properly tapped into brings all great abundance to you. Miracles, spontaneous healings, manifesting physical objects out of thin air and a great deal more can be your power, but you must be diligent in always staying connected and realizing your Higher Self, which is part of The Universal Mind.

How to Know Higher Self/Creator

You come to know your Higher Self/Creator through daily diligence of mindfulness, meditation, contemplation and/or prayer. Focus with great devotion upon your Higher Self, which is part of and ultimately is Creator, with respect and humility and will you know thy Self.

Thought precedes form; therefore, you are that which you think. You are who you hang with. You are what you eat. Consider how this makes sense.

You create your reality through the choices you make every day. **Every choice.** The energies around you and held in you, beliefs, emotions and thoughts create the ego reality. If you trust in your Higher Self and think of it as much as you can daily, fill your heart with love, and continually release your conditioned negative beliefs, emotions and thoughts, then you will know true manifestation of abundance and everything good that life has to offer. You will know The Flow.

CHAPTER 5: Seven Laws of Attraction and Manifestation (Wishing Alone Is Not Enough)

We will discuss each of the Seven Laws of Manifestation in depth throughout this book. Each has a specific place in our process of the realization of our goals. It is important that we pay attention to all of them as we begin our process of manifesting the life we desire living.

Many people are familiar with The Law of Attraction from the book and film, *The Secret,* but it is just one element of the whole. Being aware of, and in tune with, all of the seven laws is essential to efficient manifestation of the flow of abundance.

Over the next few pages I am going to provide you with a brief introduction to each of the laws and how they work together.

1. Law of Pure Potentiality

Simply put, this law states that anything is possible. Even the most outlandish thing we can think of can be created because the Universe is made of the energy of Pure Potential. If you can dream it, you can manifest it into physical reality.

We are beings of energy. Our physical forms are manifestations of energy. How we create our lives; how we choose to live is an outward projection of the energies of belief that we have in ourselves, as well as the effort that we put into achieving what we think we deserve.

Our thoughts create our worlds on both the macro- and micro-cosmic levels. If you are not happy with where your life is at this current moment, now is the time to begin thinking about it differently. Focus on what you dream of achieving – what is your intention for your life? How do you want to serve mankind?

Think big – everything exists in the realm of pure potentiality. If you can imagine it, it already exists in the ethers, the subconscious. It is possible for you to manifest anything.

Step one is believing that you can.

2. Law of Intention and Desire

Within every intention and desire is the mechanics to make it happen. If you can conceive of it, you can make it happen.

Make a list of your desires or create a vision board. These tools will help to bring the concepts of your goal into everyday awareness rather than just floating around in your head. When you place them on paper, you begin a magical act of creation. You are bringing thought concepts out of the ethers and into form in the physical realm.

One of the most difficult parts of the manifesting process is that sometimes it just seems like it takes so damn long for our desires to become reality. It's easy to start thinking that your goal will never happen.

Please know that in these times, the Universe is working to help manifest your desire, but it is also bringing experiences to you to help you fully appreciate your goal when it manifests.

Think of it this way: Just because you desire something to occur in your life does not mean that at that moment, you are ready for it. Sometimes there is work that we need to do to create our better self, to fully realize and accept that we are deserving of our desire.

These moments that challenge us to grow are not the Universe saying, "You can't have your dream," they are the Universe saying, "Let me help prepare you for your outcome."

Accept that everything that happens around you occurs for a reason. Do not judge why. Release fear and raise your vibrational energy through acceptance.

At every moment of your life, you are exactly where you are supposed to be.

Your ego conditioning may "say" something different about any given situation in which you find yourself. It will say things like, "You should have taken that other job," "You should have stayed with your previous girlfriend/boyfriend/husband/wife," or "You don't have enough money saved for retirement."

Maybe there is some truth in these statements. However, it is also true that you can change any of these circumstances by creating the intention to change your circumstances and then by taking action.

3. Law of Truth

This law relates to our larger purpose to ourselves, humanity and the planet. Why are you here on this earth;> What is your purpose? There is something that you alone are here to do. What is it?

You may find clues in examining the things that interest you. What skills are you particularly good at? What things do you enjoy doing that bring value to others?

This law is not about discovering wealth, although you may very well become quite wealthy by doing what you love rather than toiling in obscurity and frustration just for a paycheck.

Choose actions that bring happiness and success to others, this will ensure the flow of happiness and success back to you. As the old axiom states, "What goes around comes around."

As humans, it is easy for us to become frustrated as we move from a reality that is anchored in the value judgments of our ego conditioning to one of connection to our Higher Selves. Do not allow these low vibrations of ego to derail you.

Remain focused on your intention. Your "reason why" will help you to see and work past temporary setbacks. They will occur. Now that you know that, you will be prepared for them.

Release negative emotions, attitudes and patterns in order to raise your vibrations.

4. Law of Detachment

Allow yourself and others the freedom to be "who you are" and "who they are." Who we choose to be should be a conscious choice that we all have a right to decide. We also have the right to change or not. Do not try to control events. Let things occur as the Universe intends them to. Everything has a purpose most of which we are not privy to. Release judgment and beliefs about yourself and others to raise your vibrations.

I had a client who would ask for signs from God that she was on the right path. She would ask for specific signs that would never come. During our intake interview, I learned that she perceived relatives who had passed on to the next life as angels and wanted her father to be the one who came forward to help her. As the hypnotic session progressed, I asked her to call for one of her angels to come help her to work through a difficult process.

After quite a few moments of silence, I asked her if anyone was coming.

She said, "No."

I then directed her to ask for God to send the appropriate angel to help her.

Within just a few seconds, she felt the presence of her grandmother and we were able to work through her connection to a higher purpose.

After the session, I asked her if she had noticed how and when she asked for a specific angel, the process was blocked, but when she asked for the appropriate angel, the process flowed. She realized that once she was working to release the wants of the ego that were surfacing, the Universe responded to her request.

For manifestation to happen, we must let go of our limited sense and our wants that come from ego and simply ask the Universe to give us what is appropriate for us. Always be respectful and say "please" and "thank you."

One of the concepts that has been instrumental in my life has been the realization of the meaning of the phrase, "With God, all things are possible."

What does it mean for all things to be possible? Does it mean only the good things that you think you deserve? If you follow this thinking, you will continually beat yourself up every time something does not go your way. You are focused on the small, immediate level of your existence rather than the much larger picture of your life. Your ego conditioning is "telling" you that things should be different than they are.

How many times have you experienced what seemed to be a negative event that you thought was going to totally derail your life? What happened? Did you get through it? I am not suggesting that it was not a difficult time. Seeing as you are here reading this book, you obviously survived. What did you learn from that experience? Did it make you stronger, wiser, or more resilient?

You probably came out of the situation with a new, wiser perspective, a new awareness of your strengths and abilities, unless you were just focused on the moment, instead of the bigger picture.

God, and our Higher Self, perceives our lives from the scale of the Infinite. We, on the other hand, try to conceive of an infinite being from a finite mindset. Until we open up and move past our fears, we get stuck in the world of ego, thinking that we know what is best for us and that things should always go our way.

From this perspective, setbacks are monumental.

From a perspective of detachment, setbacks are merely events that are telling us that the time is not yet right. There is still something for us to learn.

Ask God, "What am I to learn from this?"

The Law of Detachment reminds us to step out of fear, step away from ego conditioning and accept things as they are. It does not mean that we should not take action, it merely asks that we allow things to be as they are without judgment, without struggling with the truth.

Unity promotes this attitude with the following affirmation at the closure of their services: "Wherever I am, God is. And wherever God is, all is well."

See the world without judgment; do not harbor ill feelings toward the driver who cut you off in traffic, do not judge the actions of others as mistakes because they did not do things as you might have done them. Accept that everyone experiences life as they should experience it. After all, it is their life. We are all here to learn and grow through specific experiences.

5. Law of Giving and Receiving

Is this a "lesson or a blessin'?" See all things that occur as gifts. It is easy to see the good things as gifts, those people and experiences that are in accordance with our perception of our wants; but what about those things that do not go how we want them to? What about our perceived setbacks? Those too are gifts. Do not view them from the small stage of your ego-mindset; view them from a higher perspective. All things occur for a reason. What can you learn from them?

Giving and receiving is The Flow of Abundance. It must be viewed from a larger point of view. When we learn from our mistakes, setbacks, and the blockages along our path, we can release ego conditioning and begin to realize our True and Higher Selves through which The Flow streams. You are then able to understand how to change karma and to release pain of all kinds to raise your vibrations. Forgive and let go. Practice acceptance.

This law also includes tithing. It is part of balance to allow flow. When you receive a financial award (income, monetary gift, lottery win), it is suggested that you give 10% of the income amount to the place where you receive your "spiritual food."

This does not necessarily mean through a church. It means anywhere that you feel the spirit of the Universe at work in your life. In Edwene Gaines' book, *The Four Spiritual Laws of Prosperity*, she describes donating to a waitress who comforted her in a time of need as she sat in a restaurant drinking coffee and contemplating a difficult experience. She felt the Hand of God present in this encounter and presented a tithe in the form of a large tip to this waitress.

Giving and receiving is one action. It is a flow. What you send out comes back to you; whether it is good thoughts, love, money, material gifts or support of any type. It is all energy. The energy is perceived by The Universe and returned. This is cause and effect at work.

It is crucial to remember your intent. If your intent behind the action is not without ego conditions, you will not get something stellar in return, because intention is the energy within the action. If there are ego desires and conditions involved in the action, it will change what is returned to you. An example: begrudgingly agreeing to help someone move to a new home will only get you some cold beer and pizza, but no support or help from The Universe.

The lower vibrations of the intent of your thoughts and feelings involved in this action, "I do not really want to do this, but he is my friend so I guess I have to," will direct the Universe to return the same low vibration, low payoff, back to you.

In other words, if you feel obliged to give your least effort, the Universe will respond with Its least effort.

"No one has ever become poor by giving." —Anne Frank

6. Law of Least Effort

Know that all people, situations and events in your life are occurring exactly as they should be.

This is known as The Flow.

Take responsibility for your situation and for all the events that you see as problems – you created and attracted them to you.

Instead of seeing blockages and challenges, perceive opportunities; choose to be gracious and appreciative of all things that are present in your life. You are exactly where you need to be at any moment.

Whether you know it or not, you have brought yourself to this exact moment in time. You did not get here by the actions of mysterious forces. All the events you have experienced and the choices that you have made in your life, (we will not judge them as good or bad, they are just choices) led to other events and more choices. Those threads of occurrences have woven the tapestry of your life.

Gracefully know that you are right where you need to be.

Take a moment and personally realize that and take responsibility for it.

You may not like your current circumstances, but you have learned a lot of things in the process of getting to where you are. Express gratitude to God for seeing you to this place. You are alive and you have a vision for what your life can be.

Once you accept your position with grace, you are ready to move forward to success.

To move forward, you must fully realize this actuality and take responsibility for your current situation. Denial will not help you to move forward. With great respect and gratitude, thank the Universe for bringing you to this place. From acceptance and acknowledgment of what currently exists you can move forward to change your reality.

Remember, no matter how extreme your circumstances may seem, you created them and you can change them.

Start now.

Let go of your need to defend your point of view. Release your ego-self entirely, that need to be right, the roles that you play and the ego version of the dream of "reality out there." Surrender it all to Divine Will so that you can raise your vibrations.

7. Law of Vibration (AKA: The Law of Attraction)

When all our energy chakras are vibrating in harmony, we realize the energy to manifest our dreams. When you first visualize your goal, you may not "feel" it as a reality. It may just be a picture in your mind. As you attune with the vibration of this image, you will be led to feel your vision around you as though it was already a reality.

How will you feel when your dream is manifested? How is that different from your feelings now? What will your life be like when you are successful? What does success feel like?

Allow yourself to feel that sense of flow and see it happening now. Step into The Flow; accept it as though your goal existed RIGHT NOW. Feel this higher vibration and live your life at this vibrational level. By doing so, you will attract the tools you require in order to realize the physical manifestation of your vision.

Some people may call this "fake it before you make it" or pretending. That is a fair assessment.

Begin to project the life you want and you can realize it. As you begin to see yourself in this light, and others begin to perceive it as well, you will find that what was once a role of pretending has become your reality.

CHAPTER 6: How Do Your Emotions Block You From Your Success?

To move forward with success, we must know which emotions are driving us.

Yes, hope is probably at the surface: hope for a better life, hope for peace, and hope for happiness.

However, ask yourself these questions, "Have I been here before? Have I felt hope, had a dream of what I want my life to be, but it did not (or never seems to) work out?

That is because there was another, stronger emotion working on a subconscious level. Your subconscious mind will never allow you to become that which you resent.

Resentment, along with fear, are very strong emotions. They also both tend to run beneath our conscious awareness.

These are deep-seated emotions that are grounded in our ego-mind. They are tied to the sense of lack that has been drilled into us throughout our lives with messages of how we are not good enough, that we cannot succeed, that we are weak, or that we will fail.

What we have learned from this is that the strongest emotion will always win. This is one of the Universal Laws of Manifesting.

If you feel happy and joyous at the thought of actualizing your life path and succeeding at your goal, you will move forward and succeed. If, however, you consciously or subconsciously are afraid of failing, afraid of succeeding, secretly resent success or fear the responsibilities that will come with realizing your goal, then you will find ways to sabotage yourself.

Gaining a sense of security is a critical step in beginning your journey of self-actualization.

You may be familiar with Abraham Maslow's *Hierarchy of Needs* (see illustration).

Originally presented in 1943 and fully published in 1954, Maslow's theory suggests that humans will not move toward self-realization and self-actualization until certain basic needs are met. In fact, they will not move from any level until the needs of the prior level are fulfilled.

The theory is typically illustrated as a pyramid. The base of the pyramid contains our Physiological Needs – food, water, air, clothing and shelter. The basic elements required for survival. Reproduction, and sexual instinct are also included here.

According to Maslow, if these basic needs were not met, then the individual would not be able to move toward the next level, Safety Needs. This makes sense – if you are focused on hunger and thirst, or are battling the elements due to lack of clothing or shelter, your survival instinct will not be focusing on safety. It will be addressing what it needs to do to keep you alive on the most basic level.

Once they have adequate food, water, air, clothing and shelter, then the individual can begin to address their safety needs. These include security in personal health and finances.

As soon as the individual feels secure, they can begin to address their needs of Love and Belonging. Here we desire interpersonal connection, external validation of ourselves and our choices. Finding groups of like-minded people, such as co-workers, church groups, hobbyists with common interests or even following sports with a crowd all help to build our sense of belonging.

Here is where things get interesting. After Love and Belonging, the next phase of Maslow's *Hierarchy* is Esteem. As we are accepted by those around us, our belief in our acceptability within society increases. This increases our sense of self-esteem.

While this is a common pattern of how the *Hierarchy* works, external validation of ourselves is transient. When we no longer feel validated by those with whom we resonated, our self-esteem can be negatively affected unless we find our internal centering and validation through Self-Actualization.

As we believe in ourselves, we begin to look for larger goals and dream of bigger things. We realize that we are more than just how we are defined by external sources. This step of Self-Realization precedes Self-Actualization. We must realize that we have a higher calling in this life before making our dream manifest (actualization). Here is where we become aware of our ability to achieve our goals and Pure Potential.

As long as we are dwelling in the lower regions of acceptance – the need for outward displays of our worthiness, external validation of our persona (ego masks) – we are ignoring our connection to the abundance around (inside) of us. This is how we behave when we are trapped in the limited "vision" of ego conditioning.

As soon as we realize our strengths, those things which are internal and intrinsic to us which are our power, and know that they cannot be taken away from us because we are children of The Universe, then we are able to rise to greater things.

Consider how Maslow's *Hierarchy* is similar to the energies of your chakras.

The energies of our Base (or Root) Chakra are focused on security and reproduction. Our fears are rooted here: fear of lack, fear of failure, fear that we will not survive. Fear immobilizes us. It keeps us from becoming who we are meant to be in the physical plane; who we know we can be. Fear takes many forms including negative inner voices or self-talk and feelings of being an impostor.

As long as we are stuck in fear of survival, we will not move forward. Believing that you can materialize what you need to survive and trusting in your dream are the first steps in healing and energizing your Root Chakra.

As we become secure and heal the Root Chakra, we move to the Sacral Chakra. Here we begin to focus on allowing ourselves to feel pleasure without over-indulging to make up for our fears and to escape worldly pressures and stressors. With the challenges of survival behind us, we can take a breath, relax and enjoy what we have accomplished; we can take pleasure in our world.

This leads us to our third chakra, the Solar Plexus Chakra. Once we have achieved pleasure and appreciate our existence through balance between surviving and thriving, we can begin to focus on ourselves and build our concept of our own personal power. This is where we develop the concept of our personal identity or our false ego self through our inter-personal relationships and dealings while becoming more emotionally healthy.

After learning of our ego selves and expressing ourselves, we move to the fourth Chakra, the Heart Chakra. This center is the nexus between the lower and higher energy centers. When we are ready to move to this area, we begin to express love for others and open to higher concepts. Once the Heart is opened, we can move toward Self-Actualization (True Self – individual soul) and then Self-Realization (Higher Self – Oversoul).

Just as in Maslow's *Hierarchy,* when we are in survival mode it is not possible to fully strive for actualization. In the chakra system, it is impossible to open to spiritual concepts when we are completely enmeshed in lower energies and are not secure in ourselves.

With the opening of the Heart Chakra, we begin working on higher vibrational levels that are not present in the lower three chakras.

After our Heart Chakra is open, we move to the Throat Chakra where we learn to express ourselves, our truths. As we have grown through the Chakra system, we have found security and comfort, become aware of our personal power and ego identity and opened to others as we begin to network and build friends. At the Throat, we have what we need to express our personal opinions and truths. We take our realization of ourselves further and say to others, "This is who I am, this is what I believe."

Understand that this is a spiritual chakra. Here you are to realize more of the True and Higher Selves and release the false ego self, together with all things by which it has been conditioned.

Advancing to the Third Eye, or Sixth Chakra, we now begin to visualize other opportunities. We see options for ourselves and others. Some people experience clairvoyance, telepathy and other higher abilities when their Third Eye is awakened. We have become more aware. Now we are seeing ourselves and our place in the world more clearly and more truthfully. We can find our sense of purpose and begin to actualize what we want to experience in life. We are willing to see all things and accept them. We begin to know that all things are from God Consciousness, of which our Higher Self is a part. We then begin to see the "bigger picture."

When we open the Crown Chakra, we are actualizing our thoughts and ideas into emotional energy that leads to manifestation. We are open to Spirit and God Consciousness and may follow the path of enlightenment. This does not necessarily mean that we become monks and live in a monastery. It merely means that we have achieved an awareness of all possibilities, The Grand Plan (AKA: Pure Potential) and create our lives accordingly.

We are now masters of our destiny as we have surrendered the ego conditioning and realized that we are spiritual beings guided by God Consciousness.

I hope you can see how the path of awakening your Chakras mirrors Maslow's *Hierarchy*.

The main theme that I would like you to realize from this is that you will have a very difficult time reaching your potential if you are stuck worrying about survival, security or identity. Work on these lower areas first and your path to enlightenment will have a solid foundation from which to advance.

CHAPTER 7: Pure Potentiality: Everything You Can Imagine Exists. Go Get It

Where do dreams/visions come from? How did you come to have your particular vision of your best future?

In this case, I am not referring to the dreams that come while we sleep. I am discussing the goals or visions that we have for our lives; the fantasies of what we think our life should be.

Maybe it is just an image that you have had in your mind for a long time and you really are not sure exactly where it came from. Maybe your vision is an amalgam of many different stimuli that you have been exposed to over many years, but just how did that specific combination arise?

Know this: No one else has this exact picture or goal. No matter how similar it may seem to the life-path of others, this is **your unique** goal and/or purpose.

It exists in the Universe of Pure Potentiality.

What does that mean? Remember our discussion of The Laws of the Universe back in Chapter 5? This is where we start digging deeper.

Your vision exists in the field of Pure Potentiality. If you can see it, you can make it exist on this plane of reality. It means that if you can dream it, if you can visualize it, then you can realize it. You can make it happen; you can make it real. Anything, truly anything, can be manifested because all possibilities exist in the Universe of Pure Potential, an unlimited universe.

Remember Confucius and Ford? No matter what you think about your ability to achieve your goals, you are correct. That belief is what will manifest. If you think you can achieve your goal, vision or dream, you will. If you think you cannot achieve you goal, well...thanks for playing.

If you would like to think of it in spiritual terms, consider this: Do you think that God plays games with you? You may feel challenged in life from time to time, but if you believe in a loving God, do you *really* think that God is capable of teasing you? Would He/She/It dangle a proverbial carrot of a possible beautiful future in front of you and not let you taste it?

Let us just suppose that since God is absolute and infinite, that He/She/It is capable of teasing you (that is a facet of being infinite – all things are possible in the physical universe, good/bad, happy/sad, beautiful/horrific); do you really think a loving God would intentionally tease you by showing you what is possible and then not allow you to achieve it? Or that He/She/It would not supply you with the tools to manifest it?

You are being shown your potential. You choose whether or not you achieve it.

Remember when we discussed that you are a co-creator in your reality? This is the "co-" part. God will not do it for you, as you have free will. You have to show Him/Her/It that you are committed to doing your work in realizing your goals. Through doing the ground work needed, you show God that you are worthy of the goal or vision. You also show yourself that you are worthy of this and can then begin to believe in yourself. Through this belief, you begin attracting more help to realize your efforts. The speed of your manifesting will increase at each level of breakthrough.

So, what is stopping you?

Oh yeah, those limiting beliefs. You are blocking yourself because you possibly think you do not deserve this wonderful future, or maybe you do not believe that you are capable of creating and sustaining it. Fear of success can be just as powerful as fear of failure, possibly stronger. Maybe you have a different limiting belief.

No matter what, it is now time to stop holding yourself back.

When you are blocked, when you feel like your dream just cannot come true, ask yourself, "What am I doing to keep this from becoming real? What am I afraid of?"

There is a good chance that fear is holding you back: fear of failure, fear of success, fear of losing everything, fear of making a mistake, or possibly fear of being laughed at. The list is endless.

What stops us from manifesting our dreams?

It is hard work. (No one said it would be effortless, but it does not necessarily need to be difficult.)

We have unrealistic expectations.

We think we are not ready.

On some deep level, we do not feel that we deserve it. We are not worthy.

We are afraid of success or failure or both.

Ask yourself if any of these false beliefs apply to you. Quiet your mind and ask for guidance. Examine emotions as you perform your chakra meditations and clear fear and you can progress to realization.

Our deterrent may not be fear. It could be that we do not feel deserving of success or possibly that we *secretly resent success.*

That is a powerful statement and one worth exploring.

Ask yourself, "Do I resent success?"

What answer do you get?

Now ask yourself, "Do I resent successful people?"

What answer comes in reply?

Even if you answered "No" to both questions, I would like you to perform the next two exercises. You may be surprised at what is underneath your seeming acceptance.

EXERCISE 1: Imagine you are driving your car. You could be anywhere. You are just out for a relaxing drive or maybe heading to work.

You stop at an intersection.

A brand new red Ferrari pulls up in the lane next to you. It is gleaming, fresh off the showroom floor.

What are you feeling as you look at the car? Are you jealous? Are you wondering where and how the driver got the money to afford the car? Are you resentful that they have one and you do not? Did you mumble to yourself, "I wonder who he cheated to afford that?"

When you look at the Ferrari again, you notice that the driver is in his mid-twenties. He is dressed fashionably and seems to not have a care in the world as he drives his very expensive car.

The traffic light turns green. Before you can pull forward, the Ferrari jumps into gear and leaves you behind as though you did not exist.

Now what are you thinking? How do you feel about the driver? How do you feel about yourself? How do you feel about displays of success and abundance such as expensive cars, large (or multiple) homes or lavish wardrobes?

EXERCISE 2: When you have conversations with friends or family, and the topic of discussion turns to people you know who are successful, do you say things like, "You would never know they had so much money. They are so down to earth, not snotty at all."

If you do not think that, congratulations! If you do think that, ask yourself this question, "Why do I believe that successful people must be arrogant by default? Why do I see only a few as *being like me?*"

What words come to mind when you think of rich people? Are they different than the words you associate with successful people? How do you define rich versus successful? Do you see them as the same or different?

If you are sensing a difference, ask yourself, "Where does my belief that successful people must be arrogant or selfish come from?"

Whatever answer(s) are presented to you are a key to your current life. While these beliefs seem to be directed toward other people, they are also focused directly at you.

To fully step forward and change your life, you MUST release these limiting beliefs. You must see abundance as a blessing, not as a way for others to show they are better than you. You must not believe that if you received abundance that you would act in a similar negative way. You must believe that abundance will bring you to realizing a better you who is connected with his/her Higher Self. Of course, you can only realize your Higher Self when ego conditioning is surrendered for the most part. It is this conditioning that is creating the negative script that has fashioned your life so far.

Your subconscious mind will never allow you to become that which you resent.

Resentment is located in the ego conditioning. So why does your subconscious block you from achieving success? Years of exposure to negative messages of successful people as poor role models have embedded that idea into your psyche.

You have a dream for yourself of living abundantly, but when you try to achieve it, something always gets in the way to prevent that realization.

Ego conditioning may hold a desire for positive, healthy growth and happiness somewhere within the negative script. If you hold a stronger belief that being wealthy/successful is equal to being arrogant or rude, then the positive desire will be overwhelmed by this negative belief and your subconscious will prevent you from manifesting abundance in your life.

Why? How could not living in abundance make you happy?

Follow this equation:

If success equals arrogance and arrogance equals bad, then, success equals bad.

If bad does not equal happy, then the inverse of statement 1 must be true.

Therefore, not being successful equals happy.

But you say, "If I had money, I would be happy. I could help people. I would not have any problems."

Due to your ego programming, you would have different problems. Your ego conditioning would sabotage you back into your comfort zone.

You would find a new way to make yourself miserable and life would continue to always bring you challenges to overcome.

Therefore, you could lose the flow of abundance to which you were connected. You could continue to live your life just as you are right now and be able to say, "See? I told you. Nothing ever works out for me."

Let's take a look at lottery winners. In 2009, Vanderbilt Law School studied lottery winners, particularly people who won between $50,000 and $150,000. Sounds like a great windfall, right? That would solve all your money problems and give you enough to start over, right?

What the research by Paige Marta Skiba found was that winners at these levels (considered mid-level) had the same debt problems as before their win. The win just postponed their filing bankruptcy.

In a joint study by researchers at the University of Kentucky, University of Pittsburgh and Vanderbilt University Law School, similar results were found. It was discovered that big winners were more likely than small winners to file for bankruptcy three to five years after winning their jackpot. Overall, they found that within five years of winning, 5.5 percent of lottery winners declared bankruptcy.

Their negative script continued to control their behavior in the same framework of lack that had existed before their lottery wins. Without a connection to our Higher Selves, money is just something to use to get more stuff. With a connection to something larger, money is an avenue to change the world. Remember: Ego = temporary; Higher Self = eternal.

Ask yourself what are your negative habits and patterns of behavior and examine the strength of your will power. What is holding you back from achieving your dreams?

Know that you can change every one of your limiting beliefs into powerful affirmations that will lead you not only to realizing abundance, but realizing balance and happiness.

Being where you are right now resonates with a portion of your beliefs about yourself. Take responsibility for being where you are. Only by realizing that you are creating your life via this negative script and accepting responsibility for that creation, can you release yourself from the present circumstances and move forward.

The fact that you are reading this book means that there is another part of you that knows you should be living in abundance. You have that vision/dream – which means you can also manifest it.

To move forward and achieve that goal, your old limiting beliefs and the energies that support them must be changed. Instead of feeling comfortable in a place of despair and fear of change, you must begin to feel excited about new possibilities and joyous that you have the possibility to change.

This positive outlook will resonate in your Reticular Activating System ("RAS") and you will begin to discover opportunities for movement forward where before you only experienced challenges, blockages and lack.

CHAPTER 8: The Reticular Activating System:
What You See Is What You Get

The Reticular Activating System (RAS) is a cluster of nerves in our brain stem. The purpose of the RAS is to keep us safe by retaining images in our visual storage. For example, millions of years ago, it was important for early man to remember where he found food (and what that food looked like) so that he could safely feed himself and his tribe. It was also important, more-so, for him to remember threats such as what a tiger or particular snake looked like and where they may be located along his path to the food.

There was safety in learning what to fear and in knowing what to avoid. The knowledge that came from that fear was key to survival.

When we branch out of our comfort zone, we are expanding into unknown territory. Our reptilian brain does not know what is in that unfamiliar situation or space, so it cannot know what to fear. As a safety measure, it tells us to fear the exploration instead.

If we give in to this fear, we stay in our comfort zone and quietly watch our lives pass us by, thinking thoughts such as, "If only I would have done (fill in the blank)," "I wish I would have learned to (fill in the blank)," or "I was always so good at (fill in the blank)." I wanted to be a (fill in the blank), I don't know why I didn't pursue it."

How does this apply to the RAS?

For our purposes here, I am going to compare the RAS to a mental radar system. I like to look at the RAS as our "sphere of awareness." What is inside our sphere of awareness is what we tend to see and focus on.

You may have experienced the RAS without knowing it. Have you ever purchased a new car? Maybe you saw an ad on TV for it and thought, "Hey! That is the perfect car for me and no one else has one yet! I'll have the first one in town!"

A day after you make your purchase, you suddenly notice that more cars like yours are at nearly every corner. You notice the model everywhere, while just yesterday, you had not seen a single one.

Did one hundred people in your town somehow buy this type of car overnight? This is not probable.

This is our RAS at work. As soon as you made your purchase, the model of the car was inside your sphere of awareness. It was "on your radar."

What does this have to do with creating your perfect life? A lot!

What stories do you tell yourself about who you are, what you believe, what you are capable of? Not what your goals are, but what you think about yourself. Specifically, do you think you can achieve your desired goal?

Do you say the following things, or similar limiting statements, to yourself on a regular basis?

"You're so stupid."

"You can't do anything right."

"You're always wrong."

"You don't deserve anything"

"You don't know what you're doing."

If you do, what is on your radar, what is in your sphere of awareness? The answer is limitations instead of opportunity.

You see your failures more than you see your successes.

Why does this matter? It matters because these limiting beliefs are holding you back from achieving your goals by systematically robbing you of your successes. They keep you locked in your comfort zone.

Let's look at an example:

Imagine for a moment that you are a new sales executive at a large company. You've been given a particularly difficult prospect to work with (because nothing says positive support like hazing the new rep with customers that no one else could close). You take the challenge with eager excitement. You know you can prove yourself and get the sale. After some period of time, asking all the right questions, making all the right contacts, you have the opportunity to present your company's contract to the decision maker. Your boss is impressed with your progress and you ask him to accompany you to the meeting.

At the meeting, you perform perfectly. You close the sale and are congratulated by your new client. Your boss is proud but silent.

As the two of you enter the elevator to leave, your boss looks at you and says, "You know, that was great. We've been trying to get these guys on board for years. But, you know, if you would have talked about our new XYZ product, we could have added 20% to the contract. You could have sold an extra $2,000,000 in revenue."

What are you now focused on?

If you are like most people, you are now acutely aware of a perceived failure instead of your stellar success.

More importantly, what are you now telling yourself about your abilities?

Are you saying, "I did a great job that no one else could do," or are you saying, "How did I miss that? Why am I so stupid?"

Which one of these is right? Which one sounds like it is coming from your True or Higher Self and which sounds as if it is coming from your ego?

Become aware of these voices and beliefs as you proceed through this book. When you hear limiting beliefs, mentally stop yourself. Take the time to really examine where these beliefs are originating. Meditate on them and clear them through the chakra meditations presented earlier. It is imperative that you reframe these negative beliefs to positive affirmations.

Here is one affirmation that I wrote for my personal use to calm negative self-talk. I have also successfully used this sentence with clients to help them overcome negative voices. If you experience negative self talk, repeat this affirmation to yourself, "My inner voices are now positive and supportive." Repeat it daily as often as needed when you hear belittling talk in your mind.

Repeated exposure to any message will help to embed it into your subconscious. The good news is that you can re-program a negative belief system by methodically replacing negative messaging with repeated exposure to positive messages when you become aware of your patterns.

Create a positive mindset for yourself by writing journal entries every day that focus on what went right in your day. Ignore the negative, only focus on what went right and what you did successfully. Yes, it is important to learn from off-putting feedback or criticisms. They may be reflections of something that you need to deal with, of which you were not aware. However, do not hang onto these ideas and make these statements your credo. I promise you that within two weeks of starting this exercise, you will see a dramatic shift in your mindset. You will find that by acknowledging the positive things in your day, you will become more aware of opportunities in your environment. This mental shift is critical for helping you to move forward toward successfully realizing your dream.

My friend Michael Ferrarella embarked on a blogging exercise entitled "365 Days of Gratitude," which he began in 2015. By focusing on finding something to appreciate every day and then writing about it, Michael discovered a new sense of self and awareness of his growth.

Here is Michael's story, in his own words:

As of this writing, I am nearly 250 days into a project called "365 Days of Gratitude." This concept has existed for years, but I only heard about it in July of 2015. That was when my friend Ann embarked upon it, posting her series on Facebook. She was a few days into the project when I commented that I was fascinated by the concept.

Ann responded by challenging me to take on the project for myself.

"Sure, why not," I remember replying. And I did.

I determined my own structure for the Gratitude Project. Each day, I chose something about the day that I was thankful about. The idea was that, even during the most difficult or challenging day, there would be something for which to be grateful. I did not put impositions on myself about word count or content. Some days, due to social life or simple exhaustion, I did not write an entry. In such cases, the next time I wrote, that entry was given the next number in sequential order. A prime example was Day 30, which I wrote before a 3-day trip in which I did not have Internet access. Upon returning home, I wrote Day 31.

The Gratitude Project for me will be 365 actual entries, regardless of how many days it takes to write them all. I allow myself leeway for the unexpected nature of life itself, while also forcing myself to write 365 actual posts. I did not plot out the entries ahead of time. At the end of the day, I sat down and... wrote. Some entries took ten minutes; others, an hour.

With the first entry, I noticed how organically the words flowed. The first 15 posts lightly touched upon a variety of topics: coffee, my hair, superheroes, music, gardening, and sunlight. My gratitude became more specific over time: a tribute to pro wrestler

"Rowdy" Roddy Piper on the day he died; utilizing pain as a tool; analysis of various topics found in the movie "Fight Club" as it relates to specific elements of life and me personally.

When starting the Gratitude Project, I tended to be quick to anger and irritation. I allowed outside forces to have a negative effect on me and my perceptions of my day. External factors like noise on the street interrupting my sleep made me seethe. I took these things, these common elements of city living, personally. They were there to bother ME, no one else, just ME. My internal dialogue of doubt and self-questioning only fed a constant aggravation. This project was intended for me to use as a focus toward the positive. Despite being posted on Facebook, the project was really intended just for my own use. I had no expectations for it and was completely unprepared for what I've gained from the process.

In sharing so much of myself in writing, I've learned an openness that I've never known before. Gone are the masks that I used to use to appease other people. I no longer hide certain parts of myself just to make other people comfortable. Now I am Me.

This is called Authenticity. I live the Authentic Life.

Also, I've shed the "Loner" aspect of my personality. This part of me was the result of not being an open person, I lived as though I was an island, wherein I didn't need or want anyone else in my daily movements.

Becoming Authentic has taught me the value of other people. I value their presence. I seek others' assistance when I don't know what the heck I'm doing. No longer an island, I am touched and humbled by the comments left on many of my daily posts. I am told that my writing is looked forward to, or that certain topics I wrote about resonated with a reader. I still don't know how to accept compliments, but I now know how to appreciate them. The support of like-minded individuals helps to maintain a positive mindset and lifestyle.

Also, a completely unintended consequence of this Gratitude Project is that I found my writing voice. I hadn't written consistently in years, but writing is something I consider a passion. Starting the Gratitude Project, I was pursuing a return to writing -- I have far too many unfinished projects from a 10-year span -- but my scribblings at the time were uninspired. Writing regularly via the Gratitude Project created repetition, and that constant use of my talent allowed Writer Mike to make himself known.

The Gratitude Project hasn't been all smooth sailing. In one particular entry, I paid tribute to my Father, who died when I was 20. I wrote honestly about him, his particular struggles in life, and how they shaped my life journey and understanding. This piece received friction from certain blood family members, who believed that anything family-related should be kept private. I was hurt. It was on that day that I recognized that being Authentic will not always be accepted. Other members of my family were receptive to the words I wrote, as were friends and colleagues. Most importantly, I felt good about what I wrote, and I still do.

Very recently, I was hospitalized for reasons that still remain unanswered. Possibly anaphylactic shock. Possibly a food allergy. I'd never been in the hospital and my immediate reaction was a judgment: "This is horrible." But when it came time for me to write an entry for the day, I found appreciation for the experience: the helpfulness of the staff, the relative who stayed with me until my discharge, the newfound focus on my personal health and well-being.

My life has undergone a shift from my Old Self -- people and activities that no longer serve a purpose -- to my Self now. I associate myself with motivated and energetic people, while disassociating myself from people who are complainers and make excuses. I consume media - books, television, music - specifically. Instead of occupying my head with just anything, I pick sources that inspire or teach me. This means that I have less of a variety, but it's all there to prop me up.

The process has brought symptoms of anxiety as my brain struggles to maintain the status quo. Biologically, the brain likes to keep everything the same based on familiar patterns of comfort. Authenticity isn't about doing the same thing all the time. That little box I like to live in is comfortable, but doesn't allow for any personal growth or change.

To grow, I force discomfort. As I write, I disregard any thought of "Maybe I shouldn't write about this." Some people think it's emotionally weak for a man to cry; I do cry and I wrote about it. I experience physical weakness via difficulties breathing; I immerse myself in that experience and make it a day's writing topic. Yet, on days of exceptional physical or mental stress, I still find *appreciation for some element of the day or for the struggles themselves.*

Without a doubt, I know that I am a different person now than I was when I started the Gratitude Project back in July. I'm calmer. I laugh more. In fact, I laugh all the time. My friends and co-workers refer to it as "hearty" and "unique." I genuinely care about people outside of myself, in both my personal and professional lives.

My purpose in this journey, as I've written about most recently, is growing physically, mentally and spiritually. With roughly four months remaining before I write my last entry in the project, I anticipate more growth and change, both internally and externally.

The 365th day of gratitude will not end Hollywood-style, with all loose ends tied up and a definitive conclusion. Rather, I expect to take note of my changes over the entirety of the project, while looking forward to my continued evolution. Life itself is a journey of constant growth, learning and improvement. The 365 Days of Gratitude Project has helped me to embrace and enjoy this journey.

By focusing on finding something to be grateful for every day, Michael essentially re-wired his perceptions, and consequently his brain. He became more aware of the abundance of positive things around him and within himself.

This is a fantastic example of the RAS at work: as you focus on something, you become more aware of it. As we have already stated, if you focus on lack, you will sense shortages all around you; as you focus on abundance, you will see and appreciate the opportunities that abound around you. In fact, this awareness is a key component to the Law of Attraction.

If you want to bring good things and prosperity into your life, then you must begin to recognize just how much abundance already exists in your life. The trick is not to create abundance; that is ego talking. You must realize and become aware of what good already exists in your life, appreciate it and show the Universe gratitude for these blessings. When your thoughts, feelings, and your being start to vibrate at higher energy levels of gratitude and positive emotions and thoughts, you begin to attract more of these wonderful, higher vibrating experiences, things, and people into your life on a regular basis.

Chapter 9: Energy Systems: Chakras and Meditations

What tools can help us start to change our vibrations more consciously and effectively and re-wire our old limiting negative patterns of thinking and feeling which create unhealthy behavior and habits? Meditation is an exceedingly useful tool along with the practice of mindfulness of unhealthy behavior and habits. We can also purposely work on our energy via our energy centers, or chakras. *"Chakra"* is a Sanskrit word which is used to describe energy centers within the etheric body, an energetic counterpart to our physical body. Chakras are spinning energy centers which are associated with different areas of our lives, emotions and thoughts. There are seven main personal chakras aligned along the spine extending out the front and back of the energetic body, although there are many other chakra centers and gateways within the whole of our energy system. They spin at different levels of intensity, creating lower to higher vibrations from the Base Chakra ego-self, located at the first chakra, up to the higher vibration of spiritual awareness at the Crown Chakra. The chakras can become blocked by emotions, thoughts, traumas, learned behavior, addictions and more. Meditation on the chakras facilitates healing and release of these issues, enabling us to:

- charge the chakras with healing energy to release unhealthy blocks
- clear a path for life force to flow more
- restore balance of all energy and bodily systems
- experience life in the present
- re-wire the brain – from lower (ego) to middle (rational) and then ultimately to higher brain function (Higher Self)
- develop a perpetual connection with higher consciousness
- enhance spiritual development
- realize soul (True Self), Higher Self, and perhaps Enlightenment and Ascension
- allow Kundalini energy to travel upwards

Kundalini is a personal life force and female aspect of Divine Consciousness within us which rests in the Root Chakra. When it is successfully and safely awakened, Kundalini helps you along the path of healing as it burns and cuts away emotional and mental inertia and conditioning. It can assist you in your spiritual aspirations.

Warning: This must be done with the aid of a true spiritual teacher, master or shaman. If you believe that your Kundalini energy is awakened, find a qualified individual as soon as possible to help guide you through the process of healing, self-actualization, and ultimately self-realization.

If you are uncertain as to whether your Kundalini energy is moving, there are signs which often occur which cannot be explained as a medical condition.

These sensations include:

- heat traveling up your spine and hot spots somewhere in your body
- involuntary jerking of the arms and legs
- itching, twitching, tingly and crawly feelings
- difficulty in focusing, reading, remembering things
- flu-like body aches and pains but you do not become ill
- smelling burning incense, flowers or perfume when none is physically there
- feeling full of energy and life or possibly feeling blocked

When starting your work with the chakras, it is important to begin at the Base Chakra and move upward in steady progress. Do not proceed to the next chakra until you have completely acquired a good awareness of the chakra on which you are currently working.

As your Kundalini energy awakens, you may experience a variety of physical sensations until Kundalini eventually reaches the crown and stabilizes. Meditate on each of these feelings, sensations or symptoms separately from your chakra meditations. Learn from them. Each experience has a message for you in your process along your path. Kundalini energy is awakened in the Base Chakra and will begin moving up the spine to each of the chakras as you heal and release and work through issues.

The seven energy centers of the traditional chakra system are aligned along the spine of the energy body (which overlaps the astral and physical bodies) from the base of the tailbone to the top of the skull just above it.

In each energy point, your meditations will focus on the key elements of that chakra. For example, security and survival will be addressed as you open your base Chakra. This is the seat of our feelings for survival and for our sexual energy. By the time we arrive at the Crown Chakra, we will have moved through and beyond issues of security, love, attachment and self-esteem, to name a few, and have attained self-actualization and self-realization.

It cannot be stated clearly enough – *Do not proceed from a lower chakra to a higher one until you have experienced a definite opening of the current chakra you are working on. Do not work on the chakras out of order. Begin at the base and work on each at least two to three weeks before moving to the next. Do not try controlling the movement of the chakras. While doing your clearing and meditations, they should orientate properly on their own.*

No matter where you are on your journey, you may be new to these practices or you may have already begun to heal. Do this work systematically from the beginning. Incomplete or hasty work will not lead to full awareness. It could even be detrimental to your growth and health, as I have discovered during my years of working with clients who have started on their healing path on their own who had literally played or experimented with chakras only after gaining a small amount of understanding.

I will describe each of the chakras and the questions that you will focus on for each as you perform the chakra clearing meditation. Focus on these questions as you meditate on each specific chakra to gain awareness of your blockages and begin the process of letting go and discovering your True Self.

Chakras have colors which can be perceived through higher sight. The system of chakras is the spectrum of a rainbow, from red at the base to violet/deep purple at the crown.

Many cultures have a reference to chakras in their spiritual texts. There is generally a predominant color associated with each chakra, but they have been seen by some differently and are understood to have different perspectives to what each chakra relates to within an individual and their life. I will explain the system of chakras which is most often associated with Kundalini Yoga.

During the Chakra meditation, take a few extra minutes to go into one or more of the chakras to work on deeper issues. Use the questions outlined below for each energy center.

We will begin at the **Base Chakra** also known as the Root Chakra. The first chakra, is located at the base of the spine near the end of the tailbone and is a healthy blood red color. It is linked to family and fellow human beings, connection to the Earth's energy, grounded within the physical plane of existence, survival (abundance or lack thereof) and sexual energy. Kundalini energy, as previously mentioned, rests here.

Questions of focus while meditating on the First Chakra:
- What are my fears surrounding my survival?
- Spiders or snakes? Could they bite and kill me?
- Lack? Do I have a healthy safe place to live? Enough food, clothing etc?
- Can I take care of myself and provide what I need?
- What was I taught by others regarding surviving and thriving?
- Is it a "dog eat dog" world?
- Successful people only think of themselves?
- "Good guys finish last?"
- Is life a struggle?

Sacral Chakra. The second chakra is located just below the belly button. It is a vivid orange color and is linked to our inner child (repressed emotions and thoughts) and relationships which are more personal, as well as sex and procreation. Many different types of addictions and modes of behavior modification, such as shopping therapy, and eating disorders also stem from the second chakra.

Questions of focus while meditating on Second Chakra:
- What types of relationships do I have in my life?
- Are they healthy? If not, why do I keep these relationships?
- Do I understand what a healthy relationship is?
- Is co-dependency involved?
- Do I deal with my emotions?

- Do I have many repressed emotions? In other words, can I feel most emotions or do I stuff them deep down until "they go away?"
- Am I quick to anger? If so, why?
- What do I experience emotionally on a day-to-day basis?
- Do my emotions control me?
- Do I enjoy sex?
- Do I have many inhibitions?
- What was I taught about sex?
- Do I accept all sexual orientations? Am I homophobic?

Solar Plexus. The third Chakra, goes from just below the breastbone down to the navel. It is a light-yellow color and is linked to our "shoulds, woulds and coulds," self-esteem, reaction to criticism, personal power, confidence and self-respect that is ego-based conditioning.

Questions of focus while meditating on the Third Chakra:

- Do I feel empowered?
- Can I stand up for myself?
- Do I argue or discuss my viewpoints?
- Am I allowing myself to be used and/or abused?
- Am I a capable, decisive individual?
- Do I respect myself?
- Am I self-aware?
- Am I a confident individual?
- Am I worthy?

Heart Chakra. The fourth chakra, is in the center of the chest in the breast bone area. It displays as spring forest green or a very light rosy pink. It is linked to higher love, compassion, acceptance, openness, inspiration and guidance from soul and ultimately the Higher Self.

Questions of focus while meditating on the Fourth Chakra:
- Do I love myself?
- Am I a genuine individual? Honest, open, loving, compassionate, gentle, consistent?
- Can I accept myself?
- Can I connect with something within that seems more real and right?
- Who or what am I truly?
- What is soul?
- Do I feel loved?

Throat Chakra. The fifth chakra, in the Adam's Apple area of the throat, is sky blue or a turquoise blue color. It is linked to expressing and living our truth, surrendering our ego will to Divine Will, trusting our Higher Self's guidance, decision making, personal authority, and creative expression.

Questions of focus while meditating on the Fifth Chakra:
What is ego will?
- Is ego my real self?
- What desires and wants drive me?
- Am I the emotions and thoughts that I experience?
- Does my ego conditioning control me?
- What is my true self?
- Can I surrender ego emotions, thoughts and roles to find my true self?
- What is Divine Will?
- Have I found a talent or ability that puts me in "the zone?"
- Is life easy to live?
- Do things fall into place?
- Do I speak my truth?
- Do I live and speak my ego truth?
- Does my True Self speak, do and think through me?
- Do I understand the roles/personas I have identified with?

Brow Chakra. The sixth chakra is between your eyes, just above them in your forehead. It is the color of indigo and is linked to inner vision, Divine Mind intellect, discernment, wisdom, intuition, and higher intelligence.

Questions of focus while meditating on the Sixth Chakra:
- Am I willing to see the truth of the Higher Self? Of God?
- What is the truth about reality?
- What is real love?
- What is the Flow? What is synchronicity?
- Who am I?

Crown Chakra. The seventh chakra can be found just above the top of the head directly above the spine. It is violet to a deep purple and/or pure white. It is linked to our awareness of something greater, unity, devotion, and inspiration aligned with Higher Awareness.

Questions of focus while meditating on the Seventh Chakra:
- Do I believe in something bigger than life as I know it?
- Do I meditate and connect with my Higher Self?
- Do I believe there is a Universal Mind?
- What is pure awareness?
- What is unity consciousness?

Chakra Clearing Meditation

If you like, you can perform the Tree of Life meditation (found on page 52) quickly before you do this meditation, but it is not necessary. Take your time moving through each chakra. If you are able, go to our website, www.practicalmanifesting.com, to meditate along with the recording of this meditation.

Prepare yourself to sit in meditation.

Close your eyes and relax. Take a deep breath in and hold it for three seconds and release slowly, totally emptying your mind. Take another deep breath in and do the same. Focus on your breathing. Feel your diaphragm (which is in the solar plexus area) go up and down as you breathe. Feel the breath move through the body like a wave. You are very aware of your breathing. Then expand your awareness to the physical body. Be very aware that you are in the body.

Now visualize sense or feel all around you in everyone and everything a beautiful white light. This is the energy of life force, information of creation, pure consciousness. See and/or feel this light and energy flowing through your Crown Chakra. It is violet to a deep purple color. At the crown, the energy brings life, consciousness, information regarding DNA, karma, and so much more. See and/or feel your Crown Chakra moving clockwise within you as the energy opens and heals it.

The energy continues down to the Brow Chakra. This chakra is a brilliant indigo blue color, like the bluest blue jeans. This chakra is the communication center used by your personal soul and your Higher Self. At first you have glimpses of this communication through dreams, signs, omens and visions but as the Third Eye opens, your higher intuition can develop. Then the Knowing of All things can be yours, you can be guided directly by your Higher Self. Higher abilities begin here. See and/or feel your Brow Chakra moving clockwise within you as the energy opens and heals it.

The energy continues down to the Throat Chakra. This chakra is a sky blue or turquoise blue color. Through your throat, you express yourself. At first, it is ego that speaks. As we realize that ego is a false self, we learn that ego is a medley of emotions, thoughts and imprints we have been conditioned by, roles that we play to fit in the outside world. You can surrender this ego self to your Higher Self. The will of ego is released so that your Divine Will may speak, work and think through you. The soul can guide you to help you realize your inherent talents, abilities and power. See a white void within this chakra and feel the release of ego will. See and/or feel your Throat Chakra moving clockwise within you as the energy opens and heals it.

The energy continues down to the Heart Chakra. This chakra is a spring forest green or a very light rosy quartz color. Much sorrow, pain, heartache and anguish is stored here. Open the door to your heart, let go of as much as you can. Feel these feelings leaving your body. In your Heart Chakra, there is your individual soul self; your first true contact with it. Go deep inside your Heart Chakra in search of your soul self. Perhaps it sits in a beautiful cave within you or a field so green and amazing with trees and plants. When you come upon your soul, stop and sense the great compassion emanating from it. Sense the intense pure love radiating from it. You know it is the embodiment of contentment, sympathetic joy, wisdom and peace. Connect with it. Remember who you truly are. See and/or feel your Heart Chakra moving clockwise within you as the energy opens and heals it.

The energy continues down to the third chakra in the solar plexus. This chakra is a light sunshine yellow color. This is your empowerment center. This is where vitality/power is stored. As you grew up, people took your power away through use and abuse and at times you gave your power away. Therefore, much anger gets stored here. We must release this anger as it can develop into aggressive behavior and it eats up your power. Understand your limits, but focus on your strengths. Release the voices that berate and judge you. You must believe you are a deserving person who is capable, strong, and decisive. Forgive others and yourself. See and/or feel your third chakra moving clockwise within you as the energy opens and heals it.

The energy continues down to the second chakra just below your bully button. This chakra is a vivid orange color. This is your relationship, emotional and sexual center. We store much emotional baggage around the mid-section. Deal with emotions by observing and releasing them, especially the deeply repressed ones. By looking at them and not allowing them to control you, you become less reactive, more emotionally mature and stable. Your addictions will start to lessen and you may be able to stop drug abuse, alcoholism, even the need for shopping therapy. As you become emotionally mature, you will approach personal relationships in a more open, honest and in gentle ways; based on equality, as we all are in the same "ego boat." Unhealthy relationships become easier to let go of. You enjoy sex appropriately for yourself without harming yourself or others. See and/or feel your second chakra moving clockwise within you as the energy opens and heals it.

The energy continues down and moves around and up to the first chakra near the end of your tailbone. This chakra is a healthy, blood red color. This chakra is about survival and connection to Mother Earth. Many fears are stored here regarding your survival. It is about having enough to live comfortably and thrive. You have to face your fears and realize that you are safe and have all that you need and you are blessed with so much more than is necessary to thrive. You are blessed with great abundance. Mother Earth provides. You must respect her; your life depends on it. As you overcome your fears, especially those of lack, you are able to live your life more fully, and fearlessly, instead of recklessly; but with awe and appreciation. You then feel safe and secure in this world. See and/or feel your first chakra moving clockwise within you as the energy opens and heals it.

The energy continues up along the spine to the throat area where the energy flows down a channel along the right side and out the right leg and foot into the earth. Feel the flow continuously moving through you. It is healing you, releasing blocks, and connecting you with energies above and below. The energy from Mother Earth flows up your left leg and foot up the chakras to the third chakra.

Now, focus on your breathing and take a deep breath and release it slowly, center in your Heart Chakra as you do this. Feel grounded through your feet. Open your eyes when you are ready.

Soul Purpose Meditation

Please perform one of the Tree of Life Meditations beginning on page 51 and Chakra Clearing Meditation on page 98 prior to this meditation.

As you are now grounded, centered and cleared, focus on your Heart Chakra. Visualize a door that covers your Heart Chakra, open this door and see and feel the release of all that is stuck in the Heart Chakra. Do not pay any attention to what is being released. Just dump out everything that fills this chakra. If something persists and will not be let go of easily, tell yourself that you will look at the issue later to resolve it or learn from it.

Now search for the light of your soul shining from the Heart Chakra. At first, it may be difficult to see. Whether you sense the light or not, start inward into your Heart Chakra, as if you are traveling through a tunnel. As you travel along this tunnel, it will become filled with beautiful, angelic light. You are going to a heavenly realm within you, a magnificent cavern. Perhaps there are crystals, flowers, trees, a lake... You notice in the center of this cavern sits your soul self. Your soul self will appear as it wishes. Allow it to be.

You can sense/feel/see the pure love radiating from it. You can sense/feel/see the spiritual compassion streaming from it. You know it is the embodiment of contentment, joy, peace and equanimity. It is the bridge to higher wisdom and power of Pure Consciousness.

Visualize yourself sitting with your soul self as if in a movie theater in the bleachers with a huge movie screen in front of you. Ask your soul self to show you the story of your life as it is now. View this story with an open mind free of judgment or restraint. You are watching this story to learn what is or has been effective or ineffective (such as inactions, thoughts, emotions, relationships, etc.) up to this point in your life so that you can gain a new perspective of your journey in this realm. When this movie is done, thank your soul self and ask it to show you the movie of what you have come to experience, to do and to learn specific to the higher path of your journey in this realm. Again, view this story with an open mind free of judgment or restraint to gain information of your purpose that would lead you to a more auspicious life. It will show you why you have come to be of service to all and how you are to achieve this. Ask your soul self to stay connected, to be available so that you may have guidance from this, your True Self. Ask it to help you remember that this is what you are *a spiritual being born from pure mind and pure energy.* Stay sitting with your soul self and become one with it.

Center within the still-point - the all-time-no-time, all-space-no-space point in your Heart Chakra. Here, you as soul can become one with you Higher Self, The All Knowing, All Seeing Self, the I AM. Just be.

When you are ready, focus on your breathing and take a deep breath in, hold it for three seconds, release and stayed centered. Take another deep breath in, hold it for three seconds, release and feel grounded and connected to the physical realm. You are mindful, aware and in this moment here and now. Then open your eyes when you are ready.

.

CHAPTER 10: Releasing Fear:

You Must Operate Above Survival Mode

To fear is one thing. To let fear grab you by the tail and swing you around is another.

Katherine Paterson

When you are paralyzed by fear it is a sign that your first chakra is blocked; that you are living based on the low energies of mere survival and security. Your ego conditioning is in charge, not your Higher Self.

At this level, most of us tend to do things that other people want us to do, like work in a job that we dislike, because it is secure and covers the bills. Our fear of failure to survive and thrive if we were to change jobs, *"Ego forbid!"*, creates a need to find any method of making an income which keeps us from fulfilling our Divine purpose.

We allow ourselves to be mere employees in our lives instead of co-creators of our destiny.

One clue that we are operating on an ego level is that we are existing in fear. Our ego conditioning does not allow us to change, even though we know we have a higher calling to achieve. All that the ego false self "knows" is what it has experienced in this life, whether it is conducive to thriving or barely surviving.

The false self "knows" that it has been safe overall and provided for. While all the experiences in life may not have been happy, change holds the element of the unknown. The frying pan is safer than the fire, from the point of view of what is known.

When we are operating from our True Self, we experience the flow of The Universal Mind. Worries are gone, balance is experienced and we focus on prosperity instead of lack.

As you raise your vibrations through the exercises in this book, we can promise you that you will experience moments of fear as you step out of you comfort zone to achieve your next benchmark. These fears can be overcome.

<u>Dan's Lesson</u>

A few years ago, I was at a personal crossroads in my life. I was faced with a difficult emotional choice and a huge barrier. I did my best to approach the issue with a positive outlook but, in the end, I saw that I had created a large financial hurdle for myself.

During this time, I had a meeting with a lawyer. He could see that I was beating myself up for the decisions I had made. He gave me some great advice that day.

He started by saying there are no mistakes. Things happen and we have to accept that. We do what we can to affect the outcome to be the way we want it to be, but it does not always work out that way. That is not a mistake, it just is what is.

He continued, "When I go into a trial, I go in with the intention of winning for my client. Sometimes I win. Sometimes I lose. It used to be that when I lost, I was hard on myself for being a failure and I was angry. Then I learned that was a waste of energy. I was not helping myself at all to win the next case, I was dragging myself down by focusing on what I thought was a failure.

"I began looking at things as lessons. When I lost a case, I asked myself, 'What can I learn from this?' and from that simple question, I have become more peaceful and successful.

"Do not focus on your mistakes, they don't exist. Focus instead on what you can learn from this."

Take a moment now to look at events in your life that you thought were mistakes. Examine your past and present errors. Turn them around and ask, "What can I learn from this?"

Challenge your fears. What can you learn from them? Why are they there? What is underneath them? What deeper truth exists?

Quiet your mind and meditate on the fear. Ask your Higher Self for guidance; ask for a sign, one that will be obvious to you.

One important note here: do not ask for a specific sign. That is not the way the Universe works. Ask for a sign that you will recognize and leave it to God to bring you something appropriate.

When I was facing a strong blockage, and feeling a weakness in my trust in something greater than myself, I asked for a sign. At first, I asked for specific symbols. They never came.

At the guidance of my teacher, I was told to just ask and let it go.

I prayed that evening, "Dear God, please bring a sign to me that I will understand, one that I cannot miss, that will let me know that I am on the right path. Thank you."

I then let it go. I did not think about it. Nearly two weeks went by.

Then, one Sunday morning, I was home alone with some time to fill. I turned on the TV (not a normal activity for me) and looked for something to act as background noise. I found an episode of The Twilight Zone.

At the end of the episode, Rod Serling masterfully delivering his voice-over, read from Shakespeare's *Hamlet.*

"There are more things in Heaven and Earth, Horatio, than are dreamt of in your philosophy."

I turned off the episode and picked up the book that I was reading at the time, *The Four Spiritual Laws of Success* by Edwene Gaines. I read about five pages when I ran into the same quotation from Shakespeare!

My body tingled. The same quote coming within moments from two very different sources, a quote that is about the abundance of possibilities in the Universe! This was more than mere synchronicity! I knew that my sign had been delivered to me!

I thanked God for this message to me.

In that moment, my faith in a higher consciousness was confirmed. I began my journey of releasing my ego and striving to connect to my Higher Self and someday, eventually, God.

If you are feeling trapped, ask yourself why. Where are the blockages to your growth originating?

Are they coming from resentment, fear, low self-esteem or something else? We will delve into many of these limitations in the chakra chapter. Utilize the meditations to help clear these issues at the chakra level so that you can move forward toward your goals, free of the blockages of lower energies.

The goal here is to attune to our True Self and then Higher Self. When attuned to higher consciousness, we have a different perspective on our daily stresses. They tend to become small, not as encompassing and overwhelming. Through meditation, we can connect with our Higher Self with the intent of understanding our life path as a larger picture and understanding how our temporary challenges are actually preparing us for the successful realization and actualization of our vision. Look for inner guidance through contemplation, visualization and meditation. This is the way to the True Self, the Higher Self and Its guidance.

Mindfulness of Our Natures

A human being is comprised of two natures: a lower nature/lower consciousness (which we may call the lower self, ego or personality) and a higher nature/higher consciousness (which we call the higher self). They both have the faculties of thought, feeling and action, but oriented in opposite directions. Most people are uncertain as to whether their thoughts and feelings are from their lower self or from their higher self. Life is a struggle between these two natures.

Most see no difference between them.

But there is a difference! By observing ourselves, we can recognize these differences.

Scientifically speaking they have to do with the brain, its structure and functions.

Ego, or the lower self, is perpetuated through the reptilian brain. The **reptilian** brain, the oldest part of the entire brain, controls the body's vital functions such as heart rate, breathing, body temperature and balance. The reptilian brain tends to produce rigid, habitual and very reactive thoughts and actions, as they are based on the conditioning of the person. These conditioned thoughts and responses can be in constant control because most people's reptilian brain is over-worked due to stress, anxiety and fatigue.

The limbic brain records memories of behaviors that are produced from our experiences. It is the seat of the value judgments that we make. Its functioning can be based on discerning logic and it works with reality "out there" most often. It understands the activities of the higher and lower natures through the function of cause and effect. Our True Self, the little soul, utilizes this brain through which it is The Observer.

Higher nature is associated with the neocortex. It receives and stores information for decision-making and remembering. It is involved in higher functions such as sensory perception, generation of motor commands, spatial reasoning, conscious thought and language. The neocortex helps us interact with the environment. Abstract thought, imagination, and higher consciousness processes, such as higher reasoning or wisdom and grasping the truth in general as well as reality's truth, are its specialties. The neocortex is flexible and has extensive learning capacities. Through the neocortex, human cultures, societies and the collective mind are created.

The lower nature creates a "me" presence and only thinks of this perspective. Fear and all self-indulgent emotions are its means of expression, such as anger, jealousy, greed and so on.

The Higher Self thinks about "we", that we are One, a divine unit. Therefore, thoughts and actions are more conducive for the greater good. Emotions of love, compassion, kindness and happiness flow from this nature. It brings peace, acceptance, happiness and balance when we can connect to the Higher Self.

To realize our higher nature or Self, we must overcome the reptilian's brain entrenched, conditioned ways over the mind by purposefully changing the neural pathways of the brain which connect these sections of the entire brain.

Moving through this process of self-awareness, you will discover that people around you will comment on how you are changing. Most may not like it. Since you are living to manifest your goals, instead of maintaining the status-quo that brought you to your current point of frustration, they may feel uncomfortable as they remain stuck in their ego-driven worlds.

When these relationships take this turn, know that you are on YOUR correct path. Keep walking. If others choose to walk with you, enjoy their company. If they choose to remain behind, that is not your concern. Maybe someday they will find their way, but maybe they will not.

One thing is for certain: you will no longer be mired as a satellite in the orbit of their comfort zone.

Choose yourself first.

Be the CEO of your life, not the secretary of someone else's.

CHAPTER 11: Setting Healthy Boundaries

Let's not forget that the little emotions are the great captains of our lives and we obey them without realizing it.

Vincent Van Gogh

Let us discuss the second chakra.

It is located just below your belly button; its energies are concerned with your emotions, relationships and sex.

Do your emotions get the better of you? How do you react to perceived setbacks in your life? Do you immediately rail against them, accusing others, or perhaps the Universe, of conspiring against you to "keep you down?" Do you curse the setbacks and lay blame upon yourself for not knowing better, for not being good enough to have kept the setbacks from occurring in the first place? Do you blame your parents or other authority figures for how you feel about yourself, your outlook and position in life? If you are stuck in this place of tumultuous emotions and thoughts, there is a need to establish healthy, emotional maturity.

What is emotional maturity and how do you achieve it? Emotional maturity refers to your ability to understand and manage your emotions. When you become emotionally mature you are able to create the life you desire, a life filled with happiness and fulfillment. You are able to define success in your own terms, not society's terms, and you strive to achieve it. When you are experiencing lack by justifying it to yourself through feelings of not being worthy, you are vibrating at a low emotional level and therefore are not emotionally healthy. Through this, you will attract more lack.

Do you feel the need to always say yes to requests from your family or friends, even the ones that create inconvenience for you? Why? Are you afraid that if you say no, they will no longer like you; that in some way, saying no makes your plans more important than theirs, that you will seem uncaring or too self-important?

When we are emotionally immature, we are worried about how others feel about us. We believe that they will feel the way we do about ourselves, which is supported by our negatively conditioned thoughts about ourselves.

Take a few moments to examine these situations. Quiet your mind and replay the last time you were in a position to say no and wanted to, but instead chose to say yes to an inconvenient request.

How did you feel after saying yes? Did you feel awful, ashamed or guilty? Perhaps you felt angry with yourself. Why did you say yes? Was it because you did not want to feel alienated by others or feared that you might be made to feel inadequate? Did you feel that you had no other choice? What did you sacrifice by not standing up for yourself? How easy will it be for you to say yes the next time now that you have created and perpetuated this precedent so that you could avoid these bad feelings?

Write the answers to these questions down. This will be your baseline moving forward. You need to realize just how much of your power you have been giving away to others and allowing your emotions to control you. You have not set healthy emotional boundaries for yourself because you are not dealing with your emotions and instead are being reactive to situations and those around you.

Now, let us be selfish for a moment.

What? Selfish is bad? You cannot allow yourself to be selfish, other people will not like you and you will be an outcast, all alone.

No. You will not be alone. You never have been and you never will be.

Let us get rid of the myth that thinking about your needs and wants is bad. Who told you that? Your parents? Friends who wanted you to do something for them? Why would they tell you that the process of you looking out for yourself was bad? It is because they had an agenda of their own and you could help them with it. They needed to validate their existence and self-worth by imposing their needs and wants upon you.

Their process of creating guilt in you so that you would comply with their wishes is another form of emotional immaturity. Some people need to control others to get their way to be right or stronger; so that they can feel better about themselves. Maybe you do it also?

Look at your relationships. Do you feel that you are a loser, so you need to compensate to hide your weaknesses or limitations from others? Are you angry with yourself for the way in which you present yourself to others, for the roles which you find yourself playing that are not authentic?

Be honest with yourself. Write down your feelings about yourself, others and various situations in your life. You are going to move past these barriers, but in order to do so, you must be aware of them and how these emotions and beliefs affect you.

What are your close relationships like? Are you a knight trying to save the world or someone from them self? Do you step back and let them lead, doing whatever they want to do? Do you feel you are smarter, better, stronger or weaker, stupid or less than others?

How do you relate to those with whom you are sexual? We are not considering just the physical act here. Let us look at attraction, lust and flirtation as well.

Are you aggressive in your pursuit, desiring power and conquest; or are you passive, waiting for them to take notice and action because you are unsure of yourself? Are you attracted to another because lust for them is burning within you or is it a more substantial, real emotion such as love or at least true admiration?

How do you handle rejection? Do you wallow in sadness, seethe in rage, or spin in confusion? Do you take it as a learning experience or do you beat yourself up because you were not good enough/sexy enough/manly or womanly enough? Do you shrink away, telling yourself that you will never find the right partner?

How do you react to sexual activity? Do you view it as a power trip or a private matter that is not to be discussed, an act that is "dirty" instead of natural? Do you announce your conquest to your friends, basking in their recognition of your triumph, which makes you feel great about yourself? Do you internalize it and look for the next level of competition to increase your prowess? Is there true intimacy or is it shallow pleasure? Do you only think of your own emotional and physical satisfaction or the other person's as well?

When your second chakra is in balance through self-awareness and awareness of your emotions, you will learn to avoid the negative emotional approaches and reactions. You will find that your attitude toward relationships will be one of balance. Yes, people come and go in our lives, but each one is there at a given time for a purpose. Some stay longer than others and some come back for a variety of reasons; including that we attract them back to us by negative longing and desire for what was and perhaps to recapture the old feelings of being loved and wanted.

No matter what or why these people are in our lives, they are there to teach us a lesson. Their presence has purpose.

As you balance your second chakra, you will begin to sense this purpose and know that nothing is wrong with you. You will begin to accept, with grace, that everything is a process and nothing is "good" or "bad," it just is.

Our labeling of events creates much of our distress. Our perceptions of events may stem from the development, or lack thereof, of our second chakra. Perceptions are framed through emotions that control us and our reactions. We move forward and create balance by dealing with past emotions and releasing them, as they have no bearing on the present or the future.

Consider this: Imagine you are in a relationship with someone with whom you are satisfied and comfortable. Things could be better, more exciting, maybe more passionate, but you feel secure even though you feel the possibility that something better exists. Your girlfriend/boyfriend/husband/wife leaves you for someone else. How do you feel? Devastated, confused, happy?

One week later, you meet someone who is even more in balance with your goals for a happier relationship and holds similar views on life as you do. How do you feel? Confused, happy, or perhaps remorseful that you did not meet them sooner?

You may have been sad when your previous relationship ended, but the possibility of the new one cannot enter your life until the energy of the old relationship is released.

Living a life mired in comfortable complacency is the equivalent of living in Hell. It is a carrot-on-a-stick existence – always aware of the prize, but never able to reach it.

Please do not misunderstand me here. Goals are important; goals are what drive us forward. Sometimes that carrot is what we need to break free of the harness that holds us in a place of comfort, a place where we are not growing.

As long as there is growth and change in both parties involved in a comfortable relationship, there is reason to stay. As long as there is a solid foundation of real feelings of love, caring and devotion, you have a sturdy and healthy relationship.

What is emotional balance? We need to realize our capabilities and limitations, and adjust our feelings about ourselves accordingly. Learning to accept what you are good at and using those abilities to gain better self-esteem and self-respect is part of this healing and growth. You are realistically aware of yourself; you view your strengths and weaknesses without judgment. It is the breaking of the shackles made from old, erroneous emotions and beliefs about ourselves and our lives. It is trusting in the Universe to support us to achieve what we dream, and to believe in ourselves that we are both worthy and able to accomplish the work necessary to realize those dreams.

When emotionally healthy, we are able to utilize our abilities while not focusing on our limitations, thus creating a stronger sense of potential for the future. We then feel more secure in ourselves, happier about who we are, and overall more capable.

While we are on the subject of growth, let us discuss pain.

You probably know there are two kinds of pain – that which tells us we are injured and asks us to slow down or re-evaluate our process, to perhaps seek help, and that which tells us we are growing out of stagnation and our comfort zone.

What is the difference?

Pain that slows us down or stops us from proceeding forward may be asking us to allow ourselves time to heal before we move forward, like a broken bone or disease or a "broken heart."

Pain that moves us forward reminds us that we are alive and changing. Consider how you feel after a hard workout – your muscles are sore, but you know you are getting stronger. If you keep your workouts stagnant and never lift heavier weights or run faster sprints, your muscles will stop hurting as they get used to (bored with) this level of fitness. Only when you begin lifting heavier weights, running harder or farther, and pushing your endurance limits, bit by bit, will the pain return to let you know that you are growing. This does not mean if there is no pain there is no gain. It means that with every type of change, development and movement forward there will be some discomfort and perhaps pain to show us we are improving, releasing and/or being remade anew in some way.

We must realize that there is a healthy range in all this activity; we need to be aware of our physical, emotional and mental boundaries. If you are not sure what your boundaries are, there is a good chance that you may become hurt in some way. A sprained muscle, an emotional setback or a mental breakdown are all signs that you have pushed yourself too far, too hard and too fast.

What type of pain are you drawn to or, more precisely, what type of pain do you draw to yourself? Do you attract discomfort that stops you in your tracks? Do you like the feeling of this type of barrier? Do you think that this is the way things must be, that discomfort and pain always get in your way whenever you try something new? Do you allow it to derail you from your growth? Are you sabotaging your growth?

If you are getting in your own way, ask yourself why? Is it because on a deeper level you do not feel that you are worthy of feeling at peace? You are worthy to be happy.

We are all equal to each other. No one is better than another. We all have gifts and shortcomings; we all have strengths and struggles. We are all allowed to stand up for ourselves and say no to things that harm us. We need to create boundaries so that we can take care of ourselves.

A necessary part of manifestation is the creation of boundaries.

For you to be self-confident, there must also be a counterpoint of weakness. Without the weakness as a reference, the concept of confidence is moot.

To become aware of abundance, you must first become aware of lack. Being aware of lack may mean nothing more than knowing or sensing that you are aware of the concept of more. If you desire to be richer, you have a concept of the difference between poor and wealthy.

You are probably reading this book because you sense something bigger for you in this life. You sense the lack of your current position, but have not yet created the boundary to move beyond it.

Sometimes boundaries are subtle. Consider the borders between states or countries.

On one side of an imaginary line is territory A, on the other is territory B. They are indistinguishable at the point in which they meet. Unless you see a sign that points out the shift from A to B, you would not know that your right foot is in A and your left is in B.

These borders tell us where we are and where we are not. If we are traveling, they are how we know if we are on the right path to get us from our starting point to our destination. You cannot be in New York and Los Angeles at the same time – you are in one, the other, or somewhere in-between.

As you are on your journey, setting your boundaries and awakening your energies, please realize that there are no shortcuts. This is deep work.

Realize that all things happen at the proper time when you are ready. The Universe will not give us things which we cannot handle. We must be physically, emotionally and mentally healthy enough to experience the next great thing that comes into our lives.

This is one of the most critical things to remember in the process of manifesting. Things will happen when they happen and when you are ready, **not when you want them to happen.**

Understand, it is essential to have goals with time-frames so that you have a temporal benchmark. Do everything in your power to co-create the result by your desired date. If it does not happen on that day, do not beat yourself up. This shows that you have more work to do on yourself to become ready.

There is a reason that the end result has not occurred. Look inward and ask for guidance to understand what you need to learn or do prior to the manifestation of your desire.

You have not failed – consider how much groundwork you have done from the first day to the current date. You are on your way. Just keep going, do not give up.

Our conditioned desires demand instant gratification. It is cultural, a societal ego-conditioned point-of-view – we want things NOW!

Unfortunately, when we are granted things too soon, without doing the necessary work and laying the proper foundation, two things tend to happen:

1. We do not appreciate the gift; and
2. Our dream falls apart because we have not built solid foundations based on healthy emotional and mental states which is the environment where co-creation occurs.

The flow of abundance is a long-term pursuit. It will take time to manifest your goals and you have much work to do before it happens. Once the work is done and the foundation is built securely, then you will have abundance that will last.

Release the need to "Have it NOW" and allow yourself to understand that you are moving forward.

As you clear your second chakra with the exercises in this book, you will begin to relate to others and yourself in a more healthy, balanced way. You will not feel the need for immediate satisfaction which is based upon insecurity and lack.

Instead, you will appreciate the longevity of healthier relationships, emotional and mental balance and that abundance has been available to you all along.

CHAPTER 12: Center Of Power:

No Thing Outside Of You Has Power Over You

They are the weakest, however strong, who have no faith in themselves or their powers.

Christian Bovee

This chapter focuses on the energies of our third chakra: empowerment or insecurity.

Do you look toward the future for your happiness? Do you imagine yourself happy after an event has taken place in your life? "I'll be happy when I get a new job," "I'll be happy when I retire," or maybe after you reach a goal, "I'll be happy when I pay off this debt."

If that is how you view your achievement of happiness, STOP NOW!

These points in time are illusions. They are imaginary and based on ego conditioning. They also do not exist in a vacuum. This all depends on what you identify with, what beliefs you have about yourself.

Consider all the things that you are allowing to get in the way of your happiness. Is it really just your job or is it an entire string of varied stimuli, beliefs and opinions that you are *choosing* to allow to give your happiness and power away to?

Take time to contemplate that before reading further. Be honest with yourself. List all the things that you feel are holding you back from being happy. Then make a list of your beliefs regarding yourself.

Ready to move on?

Now that you have the lists, take a good look at them. With this knowledge now, literally, in-hand, is it really true that your happiness hinges on just one event changing? Do you believe you deserve to be happy?

You are responsible for choosing happiness and for empowering yourself. Happiness is internal, not external; it is not temporary or fleeting, it is enduring and timeless.

We are magnets. We attract what we think we deserve in our life. This is the power of the Law of Attraction. It works on both fronts, drawing to us that upon which we focus our attention, good or bad.

If we are miserable in a job, relationship or other situations and we do nothing to change it, then we are telling ourselves that this reality is what we deserve. Realize right now, that no matter what is going on in your life, you have the *power to make choices*.

This is empowerment. You are your own authority. For better or worse, you make the decisions in your life; learning your limitations, need for know-how, and what you are "made of." You discover your talents and capabilities. You are responsible for yourself, mentally, emotionally and physically. There can be no blame; no being a victim due to the actions of others or due to circumstances (especially when seemingly horrible things befall you). You are worthy to realize happiness and empower yourself. You have the right to make choices to realize your happiness. *Situations that are external to you only have the power over you that you give to them.*

You are NOT the situation. It is external to you. **Nothing outside of yourself has power over you unless you choose to allow it to.**

As we mature through the process of self-awareness and healing our emotional and mental baggage, we empower ourselves. We then can vibrate at higher levels of awareness and start operating through higher chakras. We realize higher states of being: peace, acceptance, loving kindness, compassion and balance as we move toward realizing our True Self and raising our vibrations to take the leap to fourth chakra consciousness.

As we have discussed, when we grow spiritually and vibrate at higher levels of awareness, we realize higher states of being and balance. Our viewpoints, those erroneous beliefs we have held about ourselves, are released.

Much like stimulus into our RAS creates our sphere of awareness, this awareness creates our reality. If we tell ourselves that we are miserable until something changes, then we will be miserable for a long time. Even when your job changes, some other external stimulus will come along to say, "Hello, I'm here to make you miserable again. Please, let me introduce your new boss."

Goodbye frying pan, hello fire!

Instead, let us reverse the frame of reference here. Let us choose to be happy and show gratitude for our current situation. Trust me, I know that it is hard to do initially. That is because you have not exercised the muscle to be fully aware and appreciative of your happiness and your gratitude for it. You, like me many years ago, have been focusing on lack and powerlessness. Your happiness and power are not in your sphere of awareness.

What things currently make you happy, including things about yourself? Write down anything, whether it brings you one second or one hour or one day of enjoyment.

As you think about these things, notice how your body feels differently in the moment. Your body is reacting to the thoughts of happiness and good ideals regarding yourself.

When you vibrate at the level of happiness, you attract happiness. That is the promise of the Law of Attraction. Profound, ongoing happiness is not a result or an effect of something external, it is a choice.

Do not look at your life and say, "I will be happy when _____." Look at your life and say, "I am NOW happy," then good things will happen for you. You will be vibrating at the level of happiness and attracting happiness into your sphere of awareness.

The next step in realizing abundance is to act as though your wish has already been granted; your dream has manifested.

As we have already discussed, you are a being of pure energy. The level at which your energy vibrates acts as a magnet to attract other things and people to you that are at the same level of consciousness and vibrations.

Remember the Law of Vibration/Attraction: See your goal as already existing. Feel it as your reality and live your life accordingly.

See yourself in your new role. How does it feel? You have succeeded – you have realized your dream. You are an empowered individual. Take a deep breath and let that feeling of power fill you and surround you. What word comes to mind for this feeling?

Write that word here: _____

We are going to use that word as a trigger to help you access these feelings of power at any time.

Pinch your thumb and middle finger tips together. This gesture is your anchor. If you have another physical gesture that you prefer to act as an anchor, you are free to use it. Maybe you prefer to pinch the web of your right or left hand or maybe you would like to tap your forearm. Any gesture that leads to a physical sensation for you is good. Note: this should be a movement that you can make in public, if necessary, that will not draw undue attention to you. When you make this gesture, we will call it "firing your anchor." It will be done in combination with saying your trigger.

Now, let us revisit that feeling of success. Allow that sense of achievement to fill you and surround you completely. Imagine yourself in your perfect future.

When you feel yourself in that place of perfection, take a deep breath and pause for a moment. As you exhale, fire your anchor and say your trigger word/phrase. You may say it silently or out loud.

Now do it again. Take a deep breath, feel the feelings of your success. Inhale deeply. As you exhale, fire your anchor and say your trigger.

Let that feeling of success wash over you. You are swimming in it, you are part of it. You are at home in this sensation. Accept it. Take responsibility for all that this new role will bring to you. Take another deep breath. As you exhale, fire your anchor and say your trigger phrase or word.

Whenever you feel disconnected from your path, stop, take a deep breath; as you exhale, fire your anchor and say your trigger. Through repetition, you will create an association that returns your feeling of success to you when you slow down, center yourself and speak your trigger.

CHAPTER 13: Open Your Heart: Forgiveness, Connection and Becoming Your True Self

If you want others to be happy, practice compassion. If you want to be happy, practice compassion. Dalai Lama

Your work is to discover your work and then with all your heart to give yourself to it.

Buddha

In our fourth chakra, our heart chakra, we are now ready to open ourselves to others and to the Universe through discovery of our True Self. This chakra is the level of connection to our network of people and to our higher consciousness.

Here is where we "open our hearts" to possibility, connect to those who resonate with us and learn to trust the Universe as we release our wishes for fulfillment.

Sounds easy, right? Learning to trust is one of the most difficult processes of manifestation.

Trust is typically outside of ego conditioning. We say that we trust others, but we look for validation of that trust. Our conditions surrounding trust are not open and entirely accepting; it is limited by the need for proof that we can trust and there never seems to be enough proof to do so. We must not be gullible, but we should not be fearful of trusting. Here you must learn to connect with and trust your True Self, your soul.

Being stuck in ego will slow your progress in manifesting your goals. Let me give you a personal example.

During the writing of this book, I experienced many days of fear. Fear so tangible that it nearly locked me up physically. Old patterns have a way of creeping back to you when you least expect them and as you grow spiritually, your ego conditioning will try to keep you attached to this plane. As we discussed before, ego conditioning is what you have learned and know.

I also discovered that instead of things getting easier as I progressed, they got harder. There are two reasons for this. One we have discussed, the Universe will observe you to see if you are truly worthy of your dream, dependent on your attitudes, behaviors, beliefs and so on. You must master your attitude toward the ego challenges, approach them with grace as a lesson to be learned, so that you can continue to grow and release their hold upon you.

The other reason is that as we expand our consciousness, the higher we go, the bigger the blocks. We have to work through our "stuff," our baggage of ego conditioning from this life and past lives that we carry with us. These are the things that we need to heal and release.

I eventually learned to live in the moment. In the present, there are no worries.

When I was running in fear mode, I was constantly concerned that I would run out of money. I had enough in the bank to sustain me for months, but I was scaring myself by imagining every unforeseen expense that would deplete my reserve cash and break me.

You know what happened?

I drew the things that I feared to me. I watched bill after bill arrive and saw my savings disappear.

I stepped back and looked at my situation. Admittedly, it is easy for me to write this now and tell you how you should think or feel, but in those moments, I was terrified. My short-term outlook was controlling my future by creating a space of lack, loss, depression and fear. I was creating a pit of despair for myself, financially and mentally.

Only by stepping back to gain perspective did I begin the process of climbing out of that pit.

How? I knew I had to gain control over my ego conditioning and understand that I was safe and that all was fine; I was in a secure place no matter what it looked like, no matter what story of lack ran through my mind. Just as in Maslow's *Hierarchy,* I needed security before being able to move further.

First, I asked myself if I was safe at this moment. The answer was yes, at this particular moment, you have enough money to pay this bill and still get by for a few more months.

I thanked my True Self for that response. My ego began protesting, "But what if......"

My True Self responded, "We'll deal with that then, if it happens."

At that moment, I realized that I had created the setbacks. They did not exist anywhere outside of my head. That fear and those ideas of lack due to my ego conditioning were on my RAS and the emotions connected to them were stronger than the dreams I had of success, stronger than the feeling of deserving the success that I had envisioned.

What can I tell you from this experience that may help you? I am not fully sure. Each of you will find your own touchstone to this story that will resonate for you personally.

Remember, the strongest emotion wins. If things do not seem like they are going in the right direction, meditate on your feelings about your goal. Do you have any deep fears of which you were not aware prior to this moment? If so, address those fears, calm them and release them. Strengthen your emotions of enthusiasm and joy that all is good now.

I can tell you that if you feel locked in fear, step back and take a deep breath. Imagine yourself untangled from the mess surrounding you and then make a plan.

This is one of the basic tenets that I teach to new scuba divers. STOP. BREATHE. THINK. ACT.

As scuba divers, we use lines and rope in the water frequently. We use them for navigation, recovery and location to name a few. While the lines are in the water, a diver runs the risk of becoming entangled in them.

Speaking from experience, one of the single most scary things is to be tangled in a line underwater and know that you have a limited amount of air to breathe in the tank on your back. It is initially paralyzing.

The worst thing to do at this moment is to spin furiously looking for the line and trying to release it. That frantic activity will have the reverse effect instead and you will only become more entangled.

Sound familiar?

When feeling trapped or entwined in events, focus on the moment. *Am I safe at this moment?* In diving, there is a rule: "Do you have air? If the answer is yes, then you have time. Everything else is secondary and can be solved with a clear head."

Only by gaining mental distance from our problem do we see ways past it.

Consider this: Imagine yourself standing at a brick wall. You are so close to it that your nose is touching it. What do you see or sense around you? What fills your periphery? Probably lots of bricks and mortar.

Continuing to walk forward will just result in your nose or face being damaged. But that is what most of us do. We keep moving forward, batting our faces or heads against the wall as we try to make something else, something better, happen.

Somewhere in our head, our ego mind is telling us that we can go through that wall. Maybe we can, but we will be a whole lot uglier looking when we make it through to the other side with a mangled face!

Imagine that you take a few steps back from the wall to gain a new perspective. Five or six feet of distance is all it should take. Now what is in your imaginary periphery? Can you see the end of the wall? Would it not be much easier to walk to the right or left to go around the wall rather than sacrificing your body trying to go through it? If you did not sense the end of the wall, keep stepping back from the problem until you do. All walls, all blockages are finite – every one of them can be walked around or leaped over. All blocks or walls can be overcome calmly when you can see your options for ways around them.

If you did not sense the end of the wall, keep stepping back from the problem until you do. All blocks or walls can be overcome calmly when you can see your options for ways around them. There are always options to choose from which will make your way around the blocks and walls easier. Give yourself the time to make the choices, free from stress. Go inside. Go into your heart chakra to connect with the wiser you; the one that can see possibilities, that knows what your purpose is in this life; that you can know the truth. This is your True Self, your soul.

Free your attention as best as you can from emotions and persistent, often fearful, thoughts. Meditate on the options. What feels right in your heart? What makes the most sense? You have *all the air in the world* to do this; relax and feel/sense/hear the truth. Let go of perceived sacrifices – make room for new growth, shed old skins or roles and open to new energies.

When it comes time to send your intent of abundance, success or whatever you wish to experience, if you have connected to your True Self to some degree, and you can strongly sense a possible outcome, then send it up to God or the Universe. Be sure to say "Please" as you ask for your intent to be fulfilled. Let your intensity and passion fill the request, but be respectful. After you have asked for the wish to be granted, say "thank you."

Hold gratitude in your heart. Imagine the energy of your intent flowing to you from God. It flows through the top of your head, through the body down into the ground and then back up through your feet to your heart. Allow it to spread out before you.

Now, let go of it and allow the Universe to bring it back to you as it is supposed to happen. Be free of judgment from ego. In Chapter 16, the entire meditation for this process is written out for you.

CHAPTER 14: Letting Go of Attachment to Outcome: Get Your Ego Out Of The Way

If you tell the truth, you don't have to remember anything.
Mark Twain
The truth needs so little rehearsal.
Barbara Kinsolver

In our fifth chakra, we let go of trying to control our destiny. Here we need to learn to have faith that all is as it should be and all is well. We are in God's Hands.

What we desire for ourselves in this life on a surface level is driven by ego conditioning. We see material things and wish to obtain them; we see heights of achievement and wish to attain them; we build our goals based on what we sense in this material, temporary world. To a degree, that is fine. It is, after all, where we exist in the physical form. The things around us give us a frame of reference and some are needed to survive and thrive.

Once you have imagined your goal, the next step is to release attachment to the outcome. Accept what and how the Universe fulfills your intent. You must appropriately align both your intent and your higher purpose. This alignment is the Truth.

What comes to you from The Universe may not exactly resemble what you had in mind when you made the request. Place your trust in Divine Will, which emerges from your Higher Self. After you are able to realize your True Self, you can start connecting with your All-Knowing, All-Seeing Higher Self. Anything is possible and your True Self will be guided along your auspicious path of abundance, love, wisdom and to be of service to All.

But first, you must release the ego conditioning that binds you to fear and ignorance. These emotions hide your true nature. The truth is that you are co-creator (True Self) with the Creator's Soul, the Higher Self, which is the one Super Soul Consciousness of all souls. Surrendering to the Divine Will of God, which works through your Higher Self, encompasses dissolving the ego reality as best as possible. Stop paying homage to the outside world and roles you play in it as being *your Self and real.*

This step can be difficult because we become lost in the idea of being physical, ego-driven individuals and we tend to operate from an "I Want" state of mind. We think that we know what is best for our lives and that we can make things happen. Let us face it, humans tend to be control freaks.

Let us also be clear on something else here – the process of letting go of attachment to outcome DOES NOT mean that you stop working toward realizing your goal. In fact, it means working smarter and harder to surrender, allowing things and people to come to you that may be conducive to you realizing your intent.

By seeing what presents itself and being open to how it may help realize your desired outcome, you could catch *the flow* of what The Universe has created for you. This is always an auspicious path. God will see how committed you are to doing what is necessary and what you are asked to do by your Higher Self, then favor will be yours. Things will fall into place easily, giving you what you need to fulfill God's wishes and, at the same time, fulfilling your own in some way as well.

CHAPTER 15: Placing Trust in The Universe: The Universe Knows More Than You Do

People only see what they are prepared to see.
Ralph Waldo Emerson

In the sixth chakra, we begin to see on higher levels. We begin to perceive and trust in something larger than our ego self.

Here is a story from a sister-in-law of Iris, who shares about her grandfather's belief in prayer and trust in God.

"He (her grandfather) used prayer to manifest and for him, nothing was too big or too small to pray for. One of my favorite stories was how there was absolutely no money and they needed gas for the car to go to Camrose (a small town in Alberta near where they lived). Grandma was totally stressed but for Grandpa, that was no problem. He believed God would provide. So he prayed and when he went outside, there was $5.00 in a tree (in the 40s, $5.00 was a lot of money!) Unfortunately, Grandpa passed away when I was only 10. I wish I could have known him as an adult and talked to him first-hand about his experiences and his thinking behind his belief that things would be provided to help him create his vision of life, whether it be gas money or the school he founded." - Diane

Trust. It is a difficult thing to do. We have learned over our lifetime here on this earth that some people just cannot be trusted. That is programmed in our RAS. We are always on alert, ready for the next attack on our goals and dreams, or upon ourselves.

Of course, we have also learned that there are people we can trust, those who support us and help lift us up when we falter.

The one thing that both groups of people have in common is that their actions are tangible. We have physical results to show us either outcome – and we are attached to either side of this coin. Our ego conditioning is "committed to being right," so we want trustworthy people to remain trustworthy in our minds while we defend our perception that untrustworthy people are just that as well. We define those persons by their actions. We are confused at times; uncertain about who knows the truth, or who to believe when both sides seem viable.

Have you ever asked yourself why you call certain people when you are feeling confused or frustrated, just as you avoid calling others at the same time? *It is because you already know the answer that you want to hear.* You know which of your friends will give you the advice that resonates with what you already feel you want to do. You want confirmation. That way, that you can justify your choice to yourself. You will tend to avoid calling those people who you know will question your decision-making path or present you with alternatives that seem not to take you where you want to go.

These choices are all coming from ego and low self-esteem. We are trying to control our outcome, while making it appear that we are allowing others to have a say in our choice. If we were confident in our decision, we would not need to call others for advice (we already knew what they were going to say anyway).

Trusting in The Universe is a little more nebulous. We do not always have immediate physical results to know that our intent, our goal is being acted upon. We may feel that we are on the right path, sense a flow or easiness to our actions and decisions, but we tend to want to experience our accomplishments on this plane now. When things do not happen immediately, we become doubtful and impatient. That is ego conditioning getting in the way again.

When you trust in The Universe, you trust your Higher Self, the greatness in you! You know the truth, the answers, the right questions to ask, the right things to do. You just have to tap into the Knowledge and Wisdom of The Universe and accept that all is proper as it is, because you co-created it that way for a reason. Your True Self and Higher Self always work as one to create what you really need for the best life experience - your path. When this happens, you realize Divine Love and Its Power - the energy of The Flow.

CHAPTER 16: Let It Be: Your Crowning Achievement, Take Action And Let Go

No individual can ultimately fail. The Divinity which descends into humanity is bound to re-gain its original state.

N. Sri Ram

Our Crown Chakra connects us to The Universe, to God Consciousness and beyond to Unity. When the Crown Chakra is open, we can know the essence of the Pure Consciousness that we are and commune with spiritual forces which are the energy and ground of existence Itself.

To this we will release our intentions to be fulfilled.

When making your request, remember to preface it with "Please."

After your wish has been sent through your crown chakra, it is in God's Hands. Be sure to say, "Thank you," as you fully release it to the Divine.

Now comes the hard part: Let it be. Forget about it.

We have a difficult time fully accepting that God is all powerful and infinite. He/She/It has much more resources available to Him/Her/It and power than we do through the limitations on this finite planet. Yet, being driven by ego conditioning, we consistently tend to worry because things are not the way we want them to be, or it is taking too long to manifest and so on.

Trust in The Universe. You will know that your request has been granted when it happens. It will be abundantly clear to you. It may not look exactly like what you envisioned, but you will recognize it, like an old friend you have not seen in many years.

Letting go of the outcome does not equal doing nothing. This is a common misconception. Letting go means that you do not try to influence the outcome by trying to force something to happen. It means that you go about your business and do the things you need to do. Do what is shown to you to do or what shows up and needs to be dealt with.

The Universe asks us to co-create – we have a responsibility to make our intentions happen.

For example, you may dream of winning the lottery, but if you do not occasionally buy a ticket, it is not going to happen.

Taking responsibility means that if you dream of being the first in your family to go to college, then you have to keep your grades up while you are in high school. It means that if you dream of building a business, you need to do the work necessary to be ready to get it up and running when The Universe sends you the opportunity to open your doors. It means that if you dream of running marathons for charity, you had better get off the couch and start moving, walking and running.

Ask the right questions to find out what The Universe wants you to do. To be worthy of the gift, you must do as you are guided but, sometimes, it is about waiting and seeing what happens.

If you are not clear on whether you should be granted something, ask The Universe. See your goal in your mind and ask, "God, if within your Divine Wisdom it is right for me to have this thing in my life, please grant it to me. Thank you."

If you are unsure of a path or direction to take while trying to prepare to receive, simply ask The Universe for a sign to let you know that you are on the right path. Ask for the sign to be something that you will clearly know and understand and will guide you along the correct path.

You can directly ask The Universe to reveal your correct path. Again, beginning with "Please," request that The Universe give you guidance to discover or choose the right path for your manifestation. "What is the right path for me to take so that I may achieve my highest Divine purpose?"

Always say "Thank you" after making any of these requests. You must show respect to demonstrate to God that you appreciate It and believe in It. Otherwise, our ego conditioning will become involved and ego has no ability or power to manifest anything. If you have surrendered ego properly, there should not be too much of a struggle to submit to the Divine Plan so that you may follow the flow of the path set out for you.

When The Universe reveals a pathway to you, or a task for you to accomplish, you must do what you are shown or told to do. This will let The Universe know that you are worthy of being granted your request. If you are not certain if your directions are coming from God or your ego, ask for confirmation with kindness and respectfulness until you are certain. Doubt, impatience, fear and other negative emotions along with negative thoughts directed toward the path in any way disconnects you from The Divine which causes a delay or a canceling out of your request. Apologize when this happens and ask again for what you desire to be manifested.

While I am inclined to say to you that achievement will not be easy, I actually want to look at that idea from two angles.

From our limited, earth-bound perspective, our ego conditioning drives us with basic wants and earthly desires. It also drives us for immediate gratification. However, being timeless, The Universe works at its own pace. Our entire lifetimes are barely a blink of an eye to God.

Of course, we are only on this planet for a short time. We feel that we have things to get done now and we may believe it is perhaps our only chance.

The real truth is that we have been placed here with a specific purpose in this lifetime. That purpose is tied to many other lives that we have lived and have yet to live. This lifetime is just one small piece in a grand puzzle that leads to our eventual return to God and Spirit - The Source.

Take one step at a time, yet many steps over many lives are needed. In some lives, we are meant to lay the roadwork for our soul; in other lives, we get to ride on that road in a grand carriage. Sometimes, we are just meant to watch the carriage ride past us so that we have an image of what to dream to hold for the future.

While we want our dreams granted to us immediately upon our thinking of them, this is an unrealistic expectation.

The truth is that all goals require work. As I mentioned earlier, The Universe asks us to be co-creators in our lives. We do not just show up to live in a new house, we also need to help build it up from the foundation in some way. You have groundwork to do.

What makes the difference between that work seeming hard and taking a long time versus it seeming like play and being easy? *One word: Attitude.*

Over the course of our lives, particularly when we are young, we develop certain beliefs about ourselves. These beliefs can be positive or negative, but they color our perceptions of what we think we deserve in this life. These are all based in ego conditioning.

These beliefs are reinforced by others around us, particularly people we see as authority figures, such as our parents, teachers and perhaps coaches and bosses. We can accept or reject these outside opinions as we will make choices based on what we believe about ourselves at that time.

If we believe we do not deserve our goals, we will struggle every step of the way. However, if we believe in ourselves and pursue our dreams with passion and a belief in our Higher Self and Divine Guidance, that same work will now be joyful and easy.

DECLARING YOUR INTENTION TO THE UNIVERSAL MIND

Please perform one of the Tree of Life meditations beginning on page 52 and Chakra Clearing Meditation on page 98 prior to this meditation. As you are now grounded, centered, cleared and aligned along a pathway up the chakras you may now send your intention, goal, or wish up to The Universal Mind.

On page 40, we covered visualizing your intended life or goal and holding this vision within yourself and the above meditation helped you to connect with your soul self and see the higher purpose of it being here. Now we will take this a step further.

Prepare a succinct and selfless (no ego emotions, thoughts or desires) intent. Here is an example, "May I realize the abundance of all things good: wealth, health, job opportunities, _____, _____ which are part of the path I have come to experience. This is done for the Greater Good of The All (God). Please and thank you."

Another way to word your intention could be, "May I reach _____ (total enlightenment, great material wealth, etc.) in this time for the Greater Good of The All (God). Please and thank you."

An intent must be written in a positive tone without the words, "no, not, I want, I need..." This is an important point. As we have discussed, when we write in a negative tone, we focus our vibrations on the thing(s) we do not want. For example, if you were to write, "Dear God, I need a job. I do not want to work at a place where I am not appreciated anymore," the focus of your vibrations is on lack...lack of respect, lack of money, lack of personal power. Instead of drawing appreciation, wealth, abundance and self-respect, you will instead continue to live in the cycle you wish to be released from.

It is extremely important that you understand this distinction. Ego conditioning, through which the physical plane is experienced, is limited. It is a comfort zone: something you know or something you expect that could happen, good or bad. This conditioning stops us from being aware of the abundance of opportunities and possibilities which exist within us.

A wonderful metaphor for this is the story of the monkey trap. In the story, a banana is placed in a hollow gourd. The opening of the gourd is large enough for a monkey to reach its hand into and grab the banana, but not large enough that the monkey can remove the banana while holding it. Focused intently on what it has in hand, the monkey will not let go of his treasure and is trapped by his small goal. He is seemingly unaware of the trees full of easily accessible bananas outside of the gourd that surround him.

Learn to let go of the things that hold you back. Step out of that comfort zone. Take a deep breath and look around you. See the abundance of opportunities and possibilities that present themselves to you once you step away from the small thoughts of ego conditioning.

Realize that a limitless universe of opportunity is available to you. Truly, anything that you can envision for yourself is possible to manifest in your life.

With that said, it is also important that you let opportunities come to you as the Universe chooses to send them. In our ego mind, we tend to be very specific, and that is alright. It is good to see your goal clearly. This is why vision boards are so effective in helping people realize their dreams. When people picture their goals clearly, building the board helps to attract what is needed to realize the dream as you take the necessary steps forward.

However, you must allow the Universe to bring your request in the way that It intends for you to receive it.

What does this mean? It means to keep it simple without demanding things or adding too many details concerning the goal. For example, "Please help me find the right house, with a fireplace, bay windows, 2 ½ bathrooms... and so on." Something like the following would be more appropriate: "I ask respectfully that You guide me to the house I am to experience at this time. I know in my heart it will be the right place and I will recognize it when the time comes. Let this be done for the Greater Good of The All (God). Please and thank you."

Sometimes we will receive exactly what we pictured, other times we will receive something similar. It is good to have a clear vision of your goal. In fact, it is absolutely necessary. However, when it comes to receiving your gift from the Universe, allow it to come in the way that it arrives. Accept it with grace and gratitude.

When you release the intent to the Universe, you must let go of expectations, outcomes and anticipation and wait to see what happens. Just forget about it and let it be. Align your soul/subconsciousness with God/Pure Consciousness by putting trust in the fact that it will come to pass as it should and it will be perfect for you, because you are part of The All.

Let us begin our meditation. Read the following paragraphs or you may download a recording of this meditation on our website.

MEDITATION: RELEASE YOUR INTENTION TO THE UNIVERSE

Prepare for and sit in meditation. Please perform the Tree of Life meditation on page 52, and at least a quick chakra clearing prior to this meditation. The chakra clearing meditation may be found on page 98.

Focus on your Heart Chakra. Go into your Heart Chakra. You are looking for the light of your soul. It will guide you deeper and deeper within, as if you are traversing your way along a tunnel filled with beautiful, angelic light. You are going to a heavenly realm within you, a magnificent cavern. Perhaps there are crystals, flowers, trees, a lake... You notice in the center of this cavern sits your soul self. Your soul self will appear as it wishes. Allow it to be.

You can sense/feel/see the pure love radiating from it. You can sense/feel/see the spiritual compassion streaming from it. You know it is the embodiment of contentment, joy, peace and equanimity.

Your soul self sits under a glorious tree. It has healthy branches filled perhaps with fruit, flowers... it is a wish-fulfilling tree. Become one with your soul self, be that pure love that you are... be that spiritual compassion that you are... you are the embodiment of contentment, joy, peace and equanimity, that is the unshakable, balanced mind.

Find yourself sitting under the wish-fulfilling tree as you become one with your soul self. You are pure love, compassion, and are at peace and are willingly accepting that you are connecting with Pure Consciousness through this tree.

Hold your intent within your heart. Pick a glowing piece of the wish-fulfilling tree and place your intent within it. This is your offering. Look upward. You can see another tunnel of light vertically running along the spine upon which your chakras are aligned. Repeat your intent in your mind three times while you are filling your offering with the pure love and all that you are as soul. Release the offering and watch it flow upward along the vertical tunnel of light.

As it moves through the Throat Chakra, surrender all ego desires, aversions and roles it plays, along with the outside world. Surrender to your Divine Will, ask it to work, think and speak through you for The Greater Good of the All. This creates a stronger bridge to Pure Consciousness allowing you, as soul, to co-create with God.

At the Brow Chakra, look up through the Crown Chakra and see your offering rising up into the most brilliant, glorious light, out into the infinite Universe. Hold deep respect and add, "Please and thank you." Your offering flows up through your Crown Chakra out into the Universe to Pure Consciousness. It is now out of sight. Allow it to also be out of mind.

Focus on your breathing and take a deep breath in, hold it for three seconds and release to allow yourself to center in the heart. Hold great gratitude and acceptance in your heart. Know that all will be manifested as it should. Take another deep breath in, hold it for 3 seconds and release and feel grounded and connected to the physical realm. You are mindful, aware and in this moment here and now. Then open your eyes when you are ready.

Remember to keep releasing the intent to the Universe anytime you think of it. When you do, be sure to add "please and thank you." You are making a request, not a demand. It is important to show respect to the Higher Consciousness that will be delivering your request to you.

Do not try to see an outcome or "to make it happen" unless you are certain that you are guided to do so by The Universal Mind. If doubt, fear or any type of emotion or thought which could cut the connection or stop the manifesting to occur comes up, apologize to The Universal Mind and state that you trust It and you know It is The Creator which knows best; again, adding with respect, "please and thank you."

Wait patiently to see what happens, always following that which you know is guidance from Universal Mind. Do what you are asked to do, no matter how uncomfortable it may be. Be open to higher thinking, to the higher knowing, while continually letting go of ego conditioning

CHAPTER 17: SUMMARY

Now that you have finished reading this book, your work begins.

Follow the course outlined in these pages and begin manifesting your ideal life.

Let's review a few key points from our journey:

1.   The Universe is Pure Potentiality. You are a child of The Universe. Therefore, you are a being of pure potential. All possibilities are open to you. You can be as successful as you choose to be.

2.   Anything you dream can be achieved, so dream big. Co-create great things for yourself and with others.

3.   By focusing on your strengths and properly dealing with any negativity around you, you can break free of the limitations that you have unconsciously placed on your life. With the proper mindset, you can realize a life of abundance.

4.   Recite your affirmations daily, or download the free hypnotic recording from our website so that you may engage your subconscious mind directly with these suggestions and begin building your positive mindset for success.

5.   You, and only you, determine your success. If you perceive blockages, step back and view them from a different perspective. What can you learn from them?

6.   Empower yourself through realizing that you are The Flow of the creating force. Through this book, you have learned what you are and what you are not.

You now know that you are a being of great power and wisdom.

Now go and succeed.

<u>Acknowledgements</u>

Iris and I would like to thank Norma-Jean Strickland for her providing her wonderful insights as our editor. Her familiarity with this topic was instrumental in guiding us to clarify our thoughts to present in the best way to you, our readers.

Thank you as well to all of the members of our Facebook groups, Practical Manifesting and Practical Manifesting Insiders. You've waited patiently with us while this book was finalized. We appreciate your faith in us.

Appreciation is also due to our many readers who gave us feedback on early drafts of this manuscript. Your suggestions helped us to make this the best possible presentation of all of the practical aspects of manifesting that are normally ignored in this genre.

Finally, with much gratitude, we would like to thank The Source for enlightening us with this idea and providing us with the tools to bring it into reality.

GUIDELINES

Chapter 1: Why Setting An Intention Is Critical to Your Success

- Why do you want to manifest your goal?
- What intention do you have for making it happen? Intention is our "Why."
- Focus on our intent is crucial or we you caught up in the details and slow down our process of manifestation.
- Focusing on the large goal makes tactics less important.
- Much like setting goals, nothing is ever final; each "crossroad" or step is merely a part in the process of continued achievement.
- Trust yourself to make the right choice for your life.
- Release self-pity and victim-hood and notion of "bad luck" and fears.
- Focus on gratitude for what you already have.

Setting Intent Visualization at the end of this chapter.

Chapter 2: How Do Affirmations Affect Manifestation?

- What does it mean to affirm something?
- Need for wording affirmations correctly.
- All of us interact with the world in one of three ways: visually, kinesthetically or auditorily. What does this mean and how do we find out our method? More importantly, why does it matter?
- The subconscious mind ignores the word "not', then focuses attention on that which we are thinking about in our conscious mind.
- Need to deal with the deeply rooted ego-driven conditions within the subconscious.
- Need to realize your True Self (soul) and Higher Self (Over-soul) – the I Am; the All-Knowing, All-Seeing part of the Soul.

Chapter 3: Grounding and Centering: Why you Must Start With Balanced Energy

- Without grounding to this plane and connecting with the Earth, it becomes easy for us to just fly off into ego ideas and not bring them down to the practical level of life.
- Meditation is a key to ground and center within.
- Meditation provides many physical, emotional and psychological benefits.
- Meditation brings harmony in creation by rewiring neural pathways, quieting the "monkey mind", to over-come "fight or flight" response, and can help us to hear our positive inner voices.
- Meditation can bring about a true personal transformation.

Preparation for meditation and Tree of Life Meditation - spiritual and non-spiritual- for grounding and centering at the end of this chapter.

Chapter 4: What Is The Relationship Between Creator, Co-Creator and You?

- What is creator in the lower and the higher sense of the word?
- We exist so it stands to reason that we are part of all existence; therefore, we are also part of the Universal Mind which can create anything, and has done so.
- "Mind over matter" is a truth, but it is higher mind that has the power over matter when ego-conditioned limitations are released.
- Because we are part of the Universal Mind, we have manifested this life and all conditions through laws, objects etc.; but choice, through ego mind, projects karmic (action) circumstances and experiences.
- Faith is needed in *ourselves*. This faith holds the power and all abilities that are within us.
- Faith is a higher energy vibration than ego mind.

- If we believe we know how something is to manifest, we block the flow of what truly is to be.
- Healing mentally, emotionally and even physically is very important to raise our energy and consciousness vibrations.
- As The Universal Mind – God Consciousness is The Creator and Christ consciousness is your Higher Self, your I Am.
- Need to focus with great devotion upon the Higher Self, which is part of and ultimately is Creator, with respect and humility to know thy Self.

Chapter 5: The Seven Laws of Attraction and Manifestation (Wishing Alone Is Not Enough)

- Law of Pure Potentiality
- Anything is possible as The Universe is made of the energy of Pure Potential.
- How we create our lives; how we choose to live is an outward projection of the energies of belief of ego conditioning.

- Law of Intention and Desire
- Within every intention and desire is the mechanics to make things happen.
- We can change any of situation by creating the intention to change it and taking action that applies.

- Law of Truth
- Why are you here on this earth; what is your purpose?
- What skills are you particularly good at?
- What things do you enjoy doing that bring value to others?
- Choose actions that bring happiness and success to others, this will ensure the flow of happiness and success to you.

- Law of Detachment

- Release judgment and beliefs about yourself and others to raise your vibrations.
- Allow yourself and others the freedom to be "who you are" and "who they are."
- We must let go of our limits of the mind and our wants that come from ego conditioning and simply ask the Universe to give us what is appropriate for us.
- We must be detached to any specific outcomes.
- We need to step out of fear and away from ego conditioning and accept things as they unfold. Practice acceptance.

- Law of Giving and Receiving

- Giving and receiving is The Flow of Abundance. They are one in the same.
- We must release ego conditioning and begin to realize our True and Higher Selves through which The Flow streams.
- Forgive, accept and let go as mental, emotional and physical energy blocks The Flow.
- What we send out comes back to us; whether it is good or bad thoughts, love, money, material gifts or support of any type it is all energy. The energy is perceived by The Universe and returned.

- Law of Least Effort

- Know that all people, situations and events in your life are occurring exactly as they are should be.
- Gracefully know that you are right where you need to be.
- Go with *the flow* of what is happening and learn and do what is congruent with The Flow.
- With great respect and gratitude, thank the Universe for what is and then we are able to work with The Universe to co-create.
- Surrender to God's Will so that to increase vibrations to match The Flow.

- Law of Vibration (AKA: The Law of Attraction)

- Tune into the higher vibrations of The Flow.
- Realize the vibration of that which is to be co-created with The Flow.

- Feel these as one higher vibration and live your life at this level of vibration.
- Project that which is wished to be manifested and live it as if it existed.

Chapter 6: How do Your Emotions Block You From Abundance?

- We must know what surface and deeply rooted emotions are driving us.
- Resentment, along with fear, are very strong emotions. They also both tend to run beneath our notice.
- The strongest emotion will always win, whether obvious or not.
- Gaining a sense of security is a critical step as we must self-actualize before we can realize our True Selves and The Flow.
- As long as we are dwelling in the lower regions of acceptance – the need for outward displays of our worthiness, external validation of our persona (ego masks) – we are ignoring our connection to the abundance around us and The Flow.
- The chakras and Maslow's Hierarchy of Self-actualization are similar in what is to be attained.

Chapter 7: Pure Potentiality: Everything You Can Imagine Exists. Go Get It

- All exists in the Universe as pure potential or possibilities.
- No one else has your exact vision or goal. No matter how similar it may seem this is **your unique** goal and/or purpose.

- Anything can be manifested because all possibilities exist in the Universe of Pure Potential, a universe of abundance.
- We are being shown our potential. We choose whether or not to achieve it.
- We all are co-creators in our realities. That is why we were given free will.
- What stops us from manifesting our goals?
- Negative scripts continued to control our behavior creating the same framework of lack.
- We can change our limiting beliefs into powerful affirmations that will lead t abundance, balance, and happiness.

Two sample exercises in visualizing how to over-come personal obstacles in the middle of this chapter.

Chapter 8: The Reticular Activating System: What You See is What You Get

- The purpose of the RAS is to keep us safe by retaining images in our visual storage to remember threats and danger.
- Our reptilian brain does not know what unfamiliar things, people and situations are. As a safety measure, it tells us to fear the unknown.
- If we give in to fear, we stay in our comfort zone and quietly watch our lives pass us by.
- What is inside of our sphere of awareness is what we tend to see and focus on. This includes old patterns of thinking and feeling most of which are negative.
- We need to take the time to examine where these negative patterns originated from to release them and live in the now.
- Create a positive mindset by focusing on what good things, people etc. come along each day.
- Only focus on the negative experiences to learn from them.

- When our thoughts, feelings along with our entire being start to vibrate at higher energy levels of gratitude and positive emotions and thoughts, we can attract wonderful and elevated experiences, things, people etc.
- We must realize and become aware of abundance, appreciate it and show the Universe gratitude for the good things that already are in our lives.

Chapter 9: Energy Systems: Chakras and Meditations

- Meditation is an exceedingly useful tool along with the practice of mindfulness of unhealthy behaviour, emotions, thoughts and habits.
- Chakras are spinning energy centers which are associated with different areas of our lives, states of mind, emotions and thoughts.
- Chakras spin at different levels of intensity creating lower to higher vibrations and can become blocked by emotions, thoughts, traumas, learned behavior, addictions and more.
- Meditation on the chakras facilitates healing and release of blocked energy and issues, clear a path for life force to flow more, re-store balance of all energy and bodily systems, experience life in the present, re-wire the brain and so much more.
- Kundalini is our personal life force and female aspect of divine consciousness within us which rests in the 1st chakra.
- The seven main energy centers of the traditional chakra system are aligned along the spine of the energy body (which overlaps the astral and physical bodies) from the base of the tailbone to the top of the skull and just above it.

At the end of this chapter is a list of the seven main chakras, their colors, characteristics, along with questions which can be used to identify energy blocks and issues. After which follows a meditation on clearing the chakras along with a meditation on discovering your soul's purpose.

Chapter 10: Releasing Fear.
You Must Operate Above Survival Mode

- When you are paralyzed by fear it is a sign that your first chakra is blocked; that you are living based on the low energies of base survival and security.
- Our fear-based ego conditioning does not allow us to change, as change holds the element of the unknown which induces fear.
- All fears can be overcome.
- Begin looking at negative experiences as lessons and learn from them.

Mindfulness of Our Natures

- A human being comprises of two natures: a lower nature/lower consciousness (which we may call the lower self, ego or personality) and a higher nature/higher consciousness (which we call the Higher Self).
- True Self is our personal soul consciousness.
- We can surrender ego striving and connect to the True Self and Higher Self.
- When we are operating from our True Self, we can experience the flow of the Universal Mind.
- Through meditation we can connect with our True Self and ultimately Higher Self with the intent of understanding our life path as a larger picture.
- The reptilian brain tends to produce rigid, habitual and very reactive thoughts and actions, as they are based on the conditioning of a person.
- The limbic brain records memories of behaviors that are produced via experiences. Its functioning can be based on discerning logic and works with reality "out there" most often. It understands the activities of the higher and lower natures through the function of cause and effect.
- Higher nature is associated with the neocortex. Abstract thought, imagination, and higher consciousness processes, such as higher reasoning or wisdom and the

grasping of the truth in general and of reality's truth, are its specialties.

- To realize our higher nature or Self, we must overcome the reptilian's brain entrenched, conditioned ways over the mind by purposefully changing the neural pathways of the brain which connect these sections of the entire brain.

Chapter 11: Emotions, Relationships and Sex: There's More To Life

- Second chakra is located just below your belly button; its energies are concerned with emotions, relationships and sex.
- If you are stuck in tumultuous emotions and thoughts, there is a need to establish healthy emotional maturity.
- Emotional maturity refers to our ability to understand and manage our emotions. - When we become emotionally mature, we are able to create the life we desire.
- When we experience lack, we are justifying feelings of not being worthy and are vibrating at a low emotional level and are not emotionally healthy and will attract more lack.
- Some people need to control others to get their way to be right or stronger; so that they can feel better about themselves.
- All our relationships, including sexually intimate ones, must be based on authentic emotions and healthy boundaries.
- When our second chakra is in balance through self-awareness and awareness of emotions, we learn to avoid the negative emotional approaches and reactions and can build healthy boundaries.
- People are in our lives for a reason. As we balance our second chakras, we will begin to sense and work with this purpose.
- Everything experienced is a process and nothing is "good" or "bad".

- We move forward and create balance by dealing with past emotions and releasing them, as they have no bearing on the present or the future.
- We need to realize our capabilities and limitations and adjust our feelings about ourselves accordingly. We must be realistically aware of ourselves and view our strengths and weaknesses without judgment.
- When emotionally healthy, we are able to utilize our abilities without focusing on our limitations, thus creating a stronger sense of potential for the future.
- There are two kinds of pain – that which tells us we are injured and asks us to slow down or re-evaluate our process, to perhaps seek help, and that which tells us we are stagnating within our comfort zone.
- In every type of change, development and movement forward there will be some discomfort and perhaps pain to show us we are improving, releasing and/or being remade anew in some way.
- Our goals are not realized when we have not built solid foundations based on healthy emotional and mental states.
- As we clear our second chakras, we will begin to relate to others and ourselves in a more healthy, balanced way. We will not feel the need for immediate satisfaction which is based upon insecurity and lack.

CHAPTER 12: Center Of Power: Nothing Outside Of You Has Power Over You

- The third chakra is about empowerment or insecurity which is based upon which ego beliefs we identify with.
- We are responsible for our happiness and for empowering ourselves.
- Happiness is internal, not external; it is not temporary or fleeting, it is enduring and timeless.
- We attract what we think we deserve in our life.
- Nothing outside of ourselves has power over us unless you choose to allow it to.

- As we mature through the process of self-awareness and healing our emotional and mental baggage we empower ourselves. We then can vibrate at higher levels of consciousness and realize higher states of being.
- We must follow our own authority, guided by Higher Self.

CHAPTER 13: Open Your Heart: Forgiveness, Connection and Becoming Your True Self

- Through the fourth chakra, we open ourselves up to others and to the Universe through discovery of our True Self, our soul.
- When we "open our hearts" to possibility, connect to those who resonate with us and learn to trust the Universe, we can realize fulfillment of all types.
- Trust typically is not easily habituated, as ego is fear-based.
- We must not be gullible, but we should not be fearful of trusting.
- We must learn to connect with and trust our True Self, soul, to allow our innate wisdom to guide us.
- Forgiveness helps to release the energies of stuck emotions, especially from the heart chakra.
- Remember, the strongest emotion wins. If things do not seem like they are going in the right direction, mediate on your feelings about your goal.
- Go into your heart chakra to connect with the wiser you; the one that can see possibilities, that knows what your purpose is in this life; to know the truth.

CHAPTER 14: Letting Go of Attachment to Outcome: Get Your Ego Out Of The Way

- In our fifth chakra, we let go of trying to control our destiny.
- We need to release attachment to outcome and accept what and how the Universe fulfills our intents and goals.

- We must appropriately align both our intents and your higher purposes.
- Surrender and trust in the Divine Will, which emerges from Higher Self.
- We are co-creators (True Self) with the Creator's Soul, the Higher Self, which is the one super soul consciousness of all souls.
- Dissolve ego reality as best as possible.
- By seeing what presents itself and continue to do the work that is necessary and being open we could catch the flow of what The Universe has created for us.
- Things will fall into place easily, giving you what you need to fulfill God's wishes, and at the same time, fulfilling your own in some way as well.

CHAPTER 15: Placing Trust in The Universe: The Universe Knows More Than You Do

- In the sixth chakra, we begin to perceive and trust in something larger than our ego self.
- We try to control the outcome of our goals and desires while making it appear that we are allowing others to have a say in our choice.
- Trusting in The Universe is a little more nebulous. We do not always have immediate physical results.
  - When things do not happen immediately, we become doubtful and impatient. That is ego conditioning getting in the way.
  - When you trust in The Universe, you trust your Higher Self, the greatness in all.
  - Your True Self and Higher Self always work as one to create what you really need and the best life experience - your path.

CHAPTER 16: Let It Be: Your Crowning Achievement, Take Action And Let Go

- Our crown chakra connects us to The Universe, to God Consciousness and beyond to unity.
- We can know the essence of the pure consciousness that we are and commune with spiritual forces which are the energy and ground of existence Itself.
- We must release our intent through the crown chakra then let it be and forget about it.
- Trust in The Universe. We will know when our goals/desires/intents have been granted when they happen. It will be abundantly clear but it may not look exactly as envisioned.
- The Universe asks us to co-create – we have a responsibility to make our intentions happen.
- Ask the right questions to find out what The Universe "wants" us to do. To be worthy of the gift, we must do what we are told/shown, and then waiting to see what happens.
- Ask The Universe for a sign to let you know that you are on the right path and whether your desire/goal/intent is appropriate.
- Request that The Universe give you guidance to discover or choose the right path for your manifestation.
- We must show respect by saying "Please and Thank you" to demonstrate to God that we appreciate It and believe in It.
- If we have surrendered ego properly, there should not be too much of a struggle to submit to the Divine Plan so that we may follow the flow of the paths set out for us.
- To make certain that our directions are coming from God or our ego- conditioning, ask for confirmation with kindness and respectfulness.
- Doubt, impatience, fear and other negative emotions along with negative thoughts disconnects us from The Divine which causes a delay or a cancelling out of your request.

- The real truth is that we have been placed here with a specific purpose in this lifetime. That purpose is tied to many other lives that we have lived and have yet to live.
- If we believe in ourselves and pursue our dreams with passion and with belief in our Higher Self and Divine Guidance, work to realize dreams will be joyful and easy and we will catch The Flow.

Meditation: Release Your Intention to the Universe

ABOUT THE AUTHORS

Daniel Olexa has been drawn to the powers of the mind for his entire life. After realizing his passion for helping others to improve their lives and his natural ability at problem solving, Daniel left the corporate world and began his studies in hypnotherapy. After completing 500 hours of training at the Institute for Interpersonal Hypnotherapy in Tampa, Florida, Daniel opened his first practice in Naples, FL. Daniel continues to empower others around the world to realize their strengths, discover The Flow, and reinvent their lives from his current office in Los Angeles, CA.

Orecia (Iris) Irene Terner originally hails from Edmonton, Alberta and now resides in Victoria, British Columbia, Canada. Iris studied under Randall Chipps, an aboriginal Medicine Man and Chieftain of the Dhididat Tribe of the Nootka people of the Pacific West Coast. Randall discovered Iris to be a natural-born shaman who would carry on his legacy. Upon completing her education through Randall's accredited integrated school, Iris has been working as a Shaman, Behavior Therapist, spiritual teacher, and Reiki Practitioner/Teacher for nearly 20 years. Iris lives The Flow which this book describes in detail.

Coming soon from Daniel and Iris:

A Pessimist's Guide to Manifesting
Shaman's Meditation and Prayer Book

58764892R00086

Made in the USA
San Bernardino, CA
30 November 2017